AF407361

LORD OF THE RINGS:

THE RETURN OF THE KING

ULTIMATE TRIVIA BOOK

TRIVIA, CURIOUS FACTS AND

BEHIND THE SCENES SECRETS

-

CREATED BY

ETERNIA PUBLISHING

Lord Of The Rings: The Return Of The King
Ultimate Trivia Book - Trivia, Curious Facts And
Behind The Scenes Secrets
By Eternia Publishing

© Eternia Publishing.
All Rights reserved.

Author: Eternia Publishing
Contact: contact@eterniapublishing.com

This eBook, together with all its parts, is protected
by copyright and should not be copied, sold or
transmitted without the expressed consent of the
author.

CONTENT

**ABOUT
THE LORD OF THE RINGS
MOVIE TRIOLOGY**

**ABOUT
THE RETURN OF THE KING**

**ABOUT
J.R.R. TOLKIEN**

Trivia, Curious Facts And
Behind The Scenes Secrets

ABOUT
THE LORD OF THE RINGS
MOVIE TRIOLOGY

"The Lord of the Rings" trilogy, directed by Peter Jackson and based on the epic fantasy novel by J.R.R. Tolkien, is a cinematic masterpiece that has left an indelible mark on the world of film and storytelling. Released in three parts between 2001 and 2003, this groundbreaking series brought Tolkien's richly imagined Middle-earth to life in a way that captivated audiences worldwide.

Set in a sprawling and meticulously crafted fantasy world, "The Lord of the Rings" transports viewers to a realm filled with elves, dwarves, hobbits, wizards, and fearsome creatures like orcs and trolls. At its heart, the trilogy is a tale of friendship, heroism, and the enduring struggle between good and evil. With its unforgettable characters, breathtaking landscapes, and groundbreaking visual effects, these films not only paid homage to Tolkien's literary legacy but also set new standards for cinematic storytelling.

In this journey through the trilogy, we will explore the captivating narrative, delve into the development of iconic characters such as Frodo Baggins, Aragorn, and Gandalf, and examine the profound themes of courage, sacrifice, and the corrupting influence of power. Join us as we embark on an epic adventure through Middle-earth, where destiny unfolds, and the fate of an entire world hangs in the balance. "The Lord of the Rings" trilogy is a cinematic saga like no other, and its impact on the world of film and fantasy is nothing short of legendary.

ABOUT
THE RETURN OF THE KING

"The Return of the King" is an epic fantasy film that stands as the crowning jewel in Peter Jackson's monumental cinematic adaptation of J.R.R. Tolkien's timeless masterpiece, "The Lord of the Rings." Released in 2003 as the third and final installment of "The Lord of the Rings" trilogy, this cinematic masterpiece takes us on a breathtaking journey through the mystical realms of Middle-earth. As the concluding chapter of this epic saga, "The Return of the King" brings together beloved characters, epic battles, and profound themes of courage, friendship, and the enduring struggle between good and evil. With its sweeping landscapes, captivating storytelling, and remarkable performances, this film remains a testament to the power of cinema to transport audiences to a world of wonder and imagination. In this introduction, we will delve into the cinematic marvel that is "The Return of the King" and explore its enduring impact on the world of film and storytelling.

ABOUT
J.R.R. TOLKIEN

J.R.R. Tolkien, whose full name is John Ronald Reuel Tolkien, was a literary luminary whose imaginative prowess and profound contributions to the world of fantasy literature have left an indelible mark on readers and writers alike. Born on January 3, 1892, in Bloemfontein, South Africa, and later moving to England, Tolkien's life journey was marked by a deep love for languages, mythology, and storytelling. His works, most notably "The Hobbit" and "The Lord of the Rings" trilogy, have captivated generations with their richly woven tapestries of mythical worlds, intricate characters, and epic adventures. This introduction sets the stage for a closer exploration of Tolkien's life, influences, and his enduring legacy in the realms of fantasy literature.

LORD OF THE RINGS:

THE RETURN OF THE KING

TRIVIA, CURIOUS FACTS AND
BEHIND THE SCENES SECRETS

TO ENSURE AN ADEQUATE NUMBER OF EXTRAS
FOR THE BATTLE AT THE BLACK GATE, SEVERAL
HUNDRED MEMBERS OF THE NEW ZEALAND ARMY
WERE BROUGHT IN. THEIR ENTHUSIASM DURING
THE BATTLE SCENES WAS SO INTENSE THAT THEY
KEPT BREAKING THE WOODEN SWORDS AND
SPEARS PROVIDED TO THEM.

-

THE FINAL SHOT OF PRINCIPAL PHOTOGRAPHY
FEATURED ARAGORN, NEWLY CROWNED, BOWING
TO THE FOUR HOBBITS. DESPITE NOT BEING
REQUIRED ON-SET THAT DAY, VIGGO MORTENSEN
INSISTED ON ATTENDING. HE IMPROVISED A
CROWN MADE OF PAPER, WHICH BECAME
INCREASINGLY ORNATE AND SILLY WITH EACH
TAKE AS CREW MEMBERS DECORATED IT. THE
HOBBIT ACTORS STRUGGLED TO SUPPRESS THEIR
LAUGHTER.

-

ON HIS LAST DAY OF PICK-UP PHOTOGRAPHY,
JOHN RHYS-DAVIES, WHO PORTRAYED GIMLI,
SUFFERED FROM CONSTANT RASHES CAUSED BY
THE GIMLI MAKE-UP. AS A GESTURE, THE MAKE-UP
DEPARTMENT ALLOWED HIM TO THROW HIS
GIMLI MASK INTO THE FIRE. HE EAGERLY SEIZED
THE OPPORTUNITY WITHOUT HESITATION.

-

BOTH ANDY SERKIS AND ELIJAH WOOD, WHO
PLAYED GOLLUM AND FRODO RESPECTIVELY,
WERE PRESENTED WITH PROP RINGS BY DIRECTOR
PETER JACKSON. EACH ACTOR BELIEVED THEY
HAD THE ONLY ONE, UNAWARE OF THE OTHER'S
GIFT.

-

THE MOVIE'S FINAL SPOKEN LINE, "WELL, I'M
BACK," IS ALSO THE LAST LINE OF THE BOOK,
MAINTAINING CONSISTENCY BETWEEN THE TWO
MEDIUMS.

-

THE TRILOGY'S FILMING CONCLUDED OVER A
MONTH AFTER THE MOVIE'S THEATRICAL
RELEASE AND THREE WEEKS AFTER THE 2004
ACADEMY AWARDS. SIR PETER JACKSON
ARRANGED FOR A FINAL SHOT OF SKULLS ON THE
FLOOR IN THE TUNNEL OF THE PATHS OF THE
DEAD, INCLUDED IN THE EXTENDED EDITION
DVD. THE IRONY OF FILMING SCENES FOR AN
ALREADY BEST PICTURE OSCAR-WINNING MOVIE
AMUSED JACKSON.

-

THE IDEA FOR KING THEODEN TO TOUCH THE
SPEARS OF HIS SOLDIERS BEFORE THEIR CHARGE
INTO BATTLE ORIGINATED FROM BERNARD HILL,
THE ACTOR PORTRAYING THEODEN.

-

SIR PETER JACKSON HAD AN UNPLEASANT EXPERIENCE WORKING WITH HARVEY WEINSTEIN AND BOB WEINSTEIN DURING THE FILM'S DEVELOPMENT AT MIRAMAX. AS A RESULT, THE SHARED CREDIT AT THE END OF THE MOVIE APPEARS OVER A PENCIL SKETCH DEPICTING A MAN FENDING OFF TWO OVERSIZED TROLLS. IN RETROSPECT, JACKSON REFERRED TO HARVEY AS A "REAL BULLY" WHO EXERTED CONTROL THROUGH "MAFIA THUGGERY." JACKSON ALSO REVEALED THAT WEINSTEIN WOULD HAVE LIKELY TAKEN THE PROJECT AWAY FROM HIM AND GIVEN IT TO QUENTIN TARANTINO. WEINSTEIN EVEN PREVENTED JACKSON FROM CASTING MIRA SORVINO AND ASHLEY JUDD, BOTH OF WHOM LATER ACCUSED HIM OF SEXUAL ASSAULT.

-

IN THE BOOK, EOWYN RIDES INTO BATTLE WITH THE ROHIRRIM, ACCOMPANIED BY MERRY, CONCEALING HER IDENTITY FROM THEM AND THE READER AS A CHARACTER NAMED "DERNHELM." SHE ONLY REVEALS HERSELF IN THE MIDST OF BATTLE WHEN SHE REMOVES HER HELMET TO CONFRONT THE WITCH-KING OF ANGMAR. HOWEVER, IN THE MOVIE ADAPTATION, BOTH MERRY AND THE AUDIENCE ARE AWARE OF EOWYN'S TRUE IDENTITY. THE FILMMAKERS MADE THIS CHANGE BECAUSE THEY BELIEVED IT WOULD BE CHALLENGING TO CONCEAL HER IDENTITY IN A VISUAL MEDIUM, AND NOT RECOGNIZING HER WOULD HAVE MADE MERRY APPEAR FOOLISH.

\-

GOLLUM IS DEPICTED MISSING HIS LEFT EAR LOBE IN THE FILM. THIS IMPERFECTION RESULTED FROM AN AIR TRAP IN THE CASTING PRESENTED TO SIR PETER JACKSON FOR APPROVAL. THE DESIGN TEAM DECIDED TO MAINTAIN THE DEFECT, AS IT RESEMBLED A BATTLE WOUND THAT GOLLUM MIGHT HAVE SUSTAINED DURING HIS PAST ADVENTURES.

\-

THE LORD OF THE RINGS TRILOGY BECAME THE MOST NOMINATED FILM FRANCHISE IN ACADEMY AWARD HISTORY WITH THIRTY NOMINATIONS, SURPASSING THE GODFATHER TRILOGY (TWENTY-NINE) AND THE STAR WARS FILM FRANCHISE (TWENTY-ONE).

-

THIS MOVIE MADE A STAGGERING 1,408% PROFIT FOR NEW LINE CINEMA ON THEIR INITIAL INVESTMENT.

-

HORSES OWNED BY THE PRODUCTION COMPANY WERE AUCTIONED OFF TO THE CAST AND CREW AFTER THE MOVIE'S COMPLETION. VIGGO MORTENSEN, WHO PORTRAYED ARAGORN, PURCHASED TWO HORSES—ONE THAT HE RODE THROUGHOUT MOST OF THE FILM AND ANOTHER FOR LIV TYLER'S RIDING DOUBLE, JANE ABBOTT.

-

ELIJAH WOOD'S REMARKABLE ABILITY TO MAINTAIN AN UNWAVERING STARE WITHOUT BLINKING CAME IN HANDY FOR THE SCENES WHERE FRODO WAS ENSNARED IN SHELOB'S WEB-LIKE COCOON.

-

VIGGO MORTENSEN, LIKE BILLY BOYD, CONTRIBUTED TO THE MUSICAL ASPECT OF THE MOVIE BY COMPOSING THE TUNE AND SINGING ARAGORN'S CORONATION SONG. THE ELVISH LYRICS TRANSLATE TO "OUT OF THE GREAT SEA TO MIDDLE EARTH I AM COME. IN THIS PLACE, I WILL ABIDE, AND MY HEIRS, UNTO THE ENDING OF THE WORLD," MIRRORING THE VERSE SUNG BY ELENDIL UPON HIS ARRIVAL IN MIDDLE-EARTH FROM NÚMENOR, AS DESCRIBED IN THE BOOK.

-

DURING THE TRILOGY'S PRODUCTION, VIGGO MORTENSEN ESTIMATES THAT HE "KILLED" EACH STUNTMAN ON SET AT LEAST FIFTY TIMES, CONSIDERING THE NUMEROUS TAKES AND ACTION SEQUENCES.

-

TO ENSURE THE SAFETY OF ACTOR DAVID
WENHAM DURING THE SCENE WHERE FARAMIR IS
DRAGGED BACK TO MINAS TIRITH ON
HORSEBACK, A RELEASE SYSTEM WAS
INCORPORATED INTO THE SADDLE. WENHAM
HELD A HANDLE IN HIS RIGHT HAND, ALLOWING
HIM TO DETACH FROM THE STIRRUP IF THE
HORSE UNEXPECTEDLY BOLTED. FORTUNATELY,
THE SAFETY MEASURE PROVED UNNECESSARY.

-

SIR PETER JACKSON, WHO SUFFERS FROM
ARACHNOPHOBIA, BASED SHELOB'S DESIGN ON
THE TYPES OF SPIDERS THAT EVOKE HIS DEEPEST
FEARS.

-

ONE OF THE SHOTS DURING THE CHARGE OF THE
ROHIRRIM INVOLVED A RIDER FALLING OFF THE
BACK OF HIS HORSE. REMARKABLY, ALL THE
SUBSEQUENT HORSES MANAGED TO AVOID
TRAMPLING HIM.

-

THE SHRIEKING SOUND PRODUCED BY SHELOB IS
A COMBINATION OF VARIOUS ELEMENTS,
INCLUDING THE SOUNDS OF A PLASTIC ALIEN
TOY, STEAM HISSES (INSPIRED BY AN INCIDENT
INVOLVING AN ALLIGATOR'S HISS DIRECTED AT
SIR PETER JACKSON'S DAUGHTER), AND THE
SHRIEK OF A TASMANIAN DEVIL.

-

ORIGINALLY, THIS MOVIE WAS INTENDED TO
CONCLUDE WITH A VOICE-OVER EPILOGUE BY
GALADRIEL, VOICED BY CATE BLANCHETT,
PROVIDING DETAILS ABOUT THE FATE OF THE
FELLOWSHIP OF THE RING AFTER THE EVENTS OF
THE FILM. HOWEVER, THE SCENES FEATURING
GIMLI AND LEGOLAS FOR THIS PURPOSE WERE
FILMED BUT ULTIMATELY EXCLUDED FROM ANY
VERSION OF THE FINISHED MOVIE.

-

BILLY BOYD'S SINGING SCENE IN THE MOVIE RESULTED FROM A NIGHT OUT AT A KARAOKE BAR WITH THE YOUNGER MALE CAST MEMBERS. CO-WRITER PHILIPPA BOYENS WAS IMPRESSED BY BOYD'S VOCAL PROWESS AND DECIDED TO INCORPORATE A SONG FOR HIS CHARACTER, PIPPIN. SHE REVIVED THE LYRICS FROM THE NOVEL, ORIGINALLY SUNG BY ALL FOUR HOBBITS, AND BOYD CREATED A TUNE FOR IT.

-

THE IMMENSE BATTLE SCENES, FEATURING OVER TWO HUNDRED THOUSAND DIGITAL PARTICIPANTS, REQUIRED AN ADDITIONAL ROOM TO BE BUILT AT WETA DIGITAL'S EFFECTS FACILITY TO ACCOMMODATE THE EXTENSIVE COMPUTER EQUIPMENT NECESSARY FOR RENDERING THE SCENES.

-

ACCORDING TO A MAGAZINE ARTICLE, SIR PETER JACKSON INITIALLY DISLIKED THE CONCEPT OF THE ARMY OF THE DEAD, FINDING IT TOO UNBELIEVABLE. HOWEVER, HE OPTED TO INCLUDE IT IN THE SCRIPT TO AVOID DISAPPOINTING DEVOTED FANS OF THE BOOK.

THE WORLD PREMIERE OF THE MOVIE TOOK
PLACE IN WELLINGTON, NEW ZEALAND, JUST FIVE
DAYS AFTER THE FINAL REEL WAS COMPLETED.
DIRECTOR SIR PETER JACKSON WATCHED THE
COMPLETED MOVIE FOR THE FIRST TIME AT THE
PREMIERE, EVEN THOUGH THE FILM WAS STILL
WET FROM DEVELOPING DUE TO TIME
CONSTRAINTS.

-

THE LIVE-ACTION ROHAN ARMY CONSISTED OF
SEVERAL HUNDRED NEW ZEALAND EXTRAS WHO
ANSWERED AN OPEN CASTING CALL FOR
INDIVIDUALS CAPABLE OF HORSE RIDING.
INTERESTINGLY, MANY OF THE PARTICIPANTS
WERE WOMEN WHO HAD TO PORTRAY MALE
RIDERS. THE ONLY FEMALE CHARACTER AMONG
THE ROHIRRIM DURING THE SIGNIFICANT
ASSAULT IS EOWYN, PORTRAYED BY MIRANDA
OTTO.

-

VIGGO MORTENSEN AND BILLY BOYD PROVIDED OFF-CAMERA SUPPORT DURING SAM'S WEDDING SCENE, PRETENDING TO BE WEDDING GUESTS TO ENHANCE SEAN ASTIN'S PERFORMANCE. DURING THE SCENE, AFTER SARAH MCLEOD THREW HER BRIDAL BOUQUET TO BOYD, MORTENSEN SURPRISED HIM WITH A PASSIONATE KISS. THIS BEHIND-THE-SCENES MOMENT, INCLUDING THE KISS, CAN BE SEEN IN THE EXTENDED EDITION DVD EXTRAS.

-

UNLIKE AN AVERAGE MOVIE WITH AROUND 200 VISUAL EFFECTS SHOTS, THIS MOVIE BOASTED AN ASTOUNDING 1,487 VISUAL EFFECTS SHOTS, SHOWCASING THE INTRICATE AND EXTENSIVE USE OF VISUAL EFFECTS THROUGHOUT THE FILM.

-

THE WORLD PREMIERE IN WELLINGTON DREW AN ENORMOUS CROWD, WITH APPROXIMATELY 100,000 PEOPLE LINING THE STREETS. THIS ATTENDANCE ACCOUNTED FOR NEARLY A QUARTER OF THE CITY'S POPULATION, DEMONSTRATING THE IMMENSE EXCITEMENT AND SUPPORT FOR THE FILM.

METICULOUS ATTENTION WAS PAID TO ENSURE THAT THE DESTRUCTION OF SAURON'S TOWER OF BARAD-DÛR DID NOT RESEMBLE THE TRAGIC EVENTS OF THE WORLD TRADE CENTER. THE TOWER WAS DEPICTED DISINTEGRATING FROM THE GROUND UP, AND THE SOUND EFFECTS WERE DESIGNED TO RESEMBLE BREAKING GLASS RATHER THAN AN EXPLOSIVE BLAST, AIMING TO AVOID ANY UNINTENTIONAL SIMILARITIES.

-

THE MOVIE HOLDS THE RECORD FOR THE HIGHEST NUMBER OF PERFECT ACADEMY AWARDS WINS, SECURING ALL ELEVEN NOMINATIONS IT RECEIVED.

-

IN THE ICONIC LIGHTING OF THE BEACONS SEQUENCE, ONE PHYSICAL BEACON WAS TRANSPORTED BY HELICOPTER TO THE TOP OF A MOUNTAIN AND IGNITED, WHILE THE REMAINING BEACONS WERE CREATED THROUGH COMPUTER-GENERATED IMAGERY (CGI), SHOWCASING THE SEAMLESS BLEND OF PRACTICAL AND DIGITAL EFFECTS.

EACH INSTALLMENT OF THE TRILOGY INCLUDES A
LINE THAT DIRECTLY REFERENCES THE MOVIE'S
SUBTITLE. IN "FELLOWSHIP OF THE RING,"
ELROND MENTIONS "THE FELLOWSHIP OF THE
RING" DURING THE COUNCIL SCENE, WHILE
SARUMAN MENTIONS "THE TWO TOWERS" IN "THE
TWO TOWERS" THROUGH A VOICE-OVER. FINALLY,
IN THIS MOVIE, GANDALF SPEAKS TO THE
STEWARD OF GONDOR, EMPHASIZING THAT HE
CANNOT DENY "THE RETURN OF THE KING."

-

WHEN FRODO IS SHOWN WRITING THE BOOK, THE
TOP OF THE PAGE MENTIONS THAT SAM WAS
ELECTED MAYOR OF HOBBITON, AS DETAILED IN
THE NOVEL'S APPENDICES. THIS SMALL DETAIL
ADDS A TOUCH OF CONTINUITY AND FURTHER
EXPANDS THE LORE OF THE STORY.

-

THE "OIL" POURED BY DENETHOR OVER HIMSELF AND FARAMIR WAS A COMBINATION OF WATER AND GLYCERIN, CREATING A GLISTENING EFFECT. HOWEVER, DUE TO THE SOAKING NATURE OF THIS MIXTURE, THE SCENE HAD TO BE FILMED IN A SINGLE TAKE TO PREVENT DAMAGE TO THE WIGS AND COSTUMES.

-

IN THE EXTENDED EDITION DVD VERSION, THE SCENE WHERE PIPPIN SEARCHES FOR MERRY AFTER THE BATTLE ON PELENNOR FIELDS WAS DIGITALLY ALTERED TO DEPICT NIGHT INSTEAD OF DAY. THIS MODIFICATION WAS MADE TO CREATE THE IMPRESSION THAT PIPPIN HAD BEEN SEARCHING FOR SEVERAL HOURS, EMPHASIZING THE DEEP FRIENDSHIP BETWEEN THE TWO HOBBITS. THE ORIGINAL EDIT, WHICH IMPLIED A SHORTER SEARCH TIME, GAVE PIPPIN'S REACTION TO FINDING MERRY A SENSE OF OVERREACTION.

-

THE THREE MOVIES WERE FILMED SIMULTANEOUSLY, ALLOWING FOR A COHESIVE AND CONTINUOUS PRODUCTION PROCESS.

THE OPENING SCENE, SHOWCASING SMEAGOL'S
TRANSFORMATION INTO GOLLUM, WAS DIRECTED
BY DAME FRAN WALSH, WHO ALSO CO-WROTE
AND CO-PRODUCED THE FILM. ORIGINALLY
INTENDED FOR "THE TWO TOWERS," IT WAS LATER
INCLUDED IN THIS MOVIE.

-

ELIJAH WOOD, PORTRAYING FRODO, HAD TO BE
WRAPPED IN A LATEX-LIKE MATERIAL TO
REPRESENT SHELOB'S WEBBING. IN A
LIGHTHEARTED COMMENT ON THE DVD, HE
HUMOROUSLY COMPARES IT TO BEING ENCASED
IN THE WORLD'S LARGEST CONDOM.

-

THE END-CREDIT PORTRAITS OF THE LEAD
ACTORS AND ACTRESSES ALONGSIDE THEIR
NAMES WERE SUGGESTED BY SIR IAN MCKELLEN.
PRODUCTION DESIGNER ALAN LEE CREATED
THESE SKETCHES BASED ON PRODUCTION
STILLS, WITH THE MOVIE PRESENTING A SUBTLE
MORPH BETWEEN THE SKETCH AND THE
ORIGINAL PHOTOGRAPH.

-

OF PELENNOR FIELDS WAS FILMED ON A VAST FIELD INHABITED BY RABBITS. TO ENSURE SAFETY FOR THE HORSES AND RIDERS, THE LOCATION HAD TO BE METICULOUSLY INSPECTED AND ANY RABBIT HOLES FILLED TO AVOID ACCIDENTS OR PILE-UPS.

-

SEAN ASTIN'S DAUGHTER, ALI ASTIN, HAD THE OPPORTUNITY TO PORTRAY SAMWISE GAMGEE'S DAUGHTER, ELANOR, IN THE FILM. SIMILARLY, SARAH MCLEOD'S DAUGHTER, MAISY MCLEOD-RIERA, PLAYED THE ROLE OF SAM AND ROSIE'S SON, FRODO.

-

A WEALTH OF INTERESTING FACTS AND NUMBERS RELATE TO THE TRILOGY'S PRODUCTION. THESE INCLUDE OVER SIX MILLION FEET OF FILM SHOT, 48,000 WEAPONS AND MAKEUP PROSTHETICS CREATED, 20,602 BACKGROUND ACTORS CAST, 19,000 COSTUMES PRODUCED, 10,000 CRICKET GAME ATTENDEES CONTRIBUTING ORC ARMY GRUNTS, 2,400 CREW MEMBERS INVOLVED, 1,600 PAIRS OF PROSTHETIC HOBBIT FEET MADE, 250 HORSES USED IN A SINGLE SCENE, 180 COMPUTER VISUAL EFFECTS ARTISTS EMPLOYED, 114 TOTAL SPEAKING ROLES, 100 REAL LOCATIONS IN NEW ZEALAND UTILIZED, 50 WARDROBE DEPARTMENT MEMBERS INVOLVED, 30 ACTORS TRAINED IN FICTIONAL DIALECTS AND LANGUAGES, AND A TOTAL OF SEVEN YEARS DEDICATED TO THE DEVELOPMENT OF ALL THREE MOVIES.

-

IN THE EXTENDED EDITION OF THIS FILM, LIV TYLER SINGS THE SONG DURING THE HOUSES OF HEALING SEQUENCE. INITIALLY RECORDED FOR THE MOVIE BUT UNUSED IN THE THEATRICAL RELEASE, THE SONG FOUND ITS PERFECT PLACE IN THE ADDED SCENE, MUCH TO THE REGRET OF SIR PETER JACKSON.

THE SCENE FEATURING ARAGORN'S ARMY ASSEMBLING BEFORE THE BLACK GATE OF MORDOR WAS FILMED IN A FORMER ARMY TRAINING FIELD LOCATED IN A DESERT. PRIOR TO FILMING, THE FIELD HAD TO BE CAREFULLY CLEARED OF UNEXPLODED MINES AND BOMBS TO ENSURE THE SAFETY OF THE CAST, CREW, AND EXTRAS.

-

SEAN ASTIN'S AUDITION FOR THE ROLE OF SAMWISE GAMGEE INVOLVED PERFORMING THE SCENE WHERE HE CRADLES THE COMATOSE FRODO AFTER HIS ENCOUNTER WITH SHELOB. HIS CONVINCING PORTRAYAL ULTIMATELY SECURED HIM THE ROLE.

-

FOLLOWING THE PREMIERE IN WELLINGTON, NEW ZEALAND, THE CITY HOSTED A GRAND PARTY, FUNDED BY THE CITY COUNCIL, WHICH LASTED UNTIL DAWN. THE CELEBRATION INCLUDED STREET PERFORMERS, OUTDOOR SCREENINGS, AN INTRODUCTION BY PRIME MINISTER HELEN CLARK, AND A SPECTACULAR MOCK-UP OF A FLYING NAZGÛL OVER THE EMBASSY THEATRE.

THE ICONIC SCENE OF FRODO AND SAM CLIMBING MOUNT DOOM WAS FILMED ON THE VOLCANO KNOWN AS RUAPEHU. DUE TO THE STEEP TERRAIN, ELIJAH WOOD AND SEAN ASTIN WERE ATTACHED TO SAFETY WIRES, PREVENTING THEM FROM SLIDING HALFWAY DOWN THE VOLCANO IN CASE OF A MISSTEP. THESE WIRES WERE DIGITALLY REMOVED IN POST-PRODUCTION.

-

DURING THE FILMING OF "THE LORD OF THE RINGS: THE FELLOWSHIP OF THE RING," THE TOWN OF QUEENSTOWN EXPERIENCED SEVERE FLOODS, HALTING EXTERIOR FILMING. TO CONTINUE PRODUCTION, THE CREW UTILIZED THE SQUASH COURT IN A LOCAL HOTEL AS AN INDOOR STUDIO SET. THIS UNEXPECTED CHANGE LED TO ELIJAH WOOD AND SEAN ASTIN HAVING TO PERFORM A PIVOTAL SCENE WITHOUT PROPER PREPARATION, WITH A CREW MEMBER STANDING IN FOR THE YET-TO-BE-CAST GOLLUM. DESPITE THE CHALLENGES, ASTIN SUCCESSFULLY COMPLETED HIS SCENES, BUT THE RETURN TO THE SQUASH COURT FOR WOOD'S SCENES WAS DELAYED DUE TO THE IMPROVED WEATHER CONDITIONS.

THE LATE SIR CHRISTOPHER LEE, KNOWN FOR HIS ROLE AS SARUMAN, HAD A PROFOUND CONNECTION TO "THE LORD OF THE RINGS." HE READ J.R.R. TOLKIEN'S EPIC TALE ANNUALLY UNTIL HIS DEATH IN 2015, MAKING HIM THE ONLY CAST MEMBER TO HAVE PERSONALLY MET THE AUTHOR.

-

IN THE EXTENDED EDITION OF THE FILM, THE HELMET WORN BY THE MOUTH OF SAURON BEARS RUNES THAT, WHEN TRANSLATED, READ "LAMMEN GORTHAUR." THIS PHRASE, MEANING "VOICE OF THE DREAD ABOMINATION," ADDS TO THE CHARACTER'S OMINOUS PRESENCE AND ESTABLISHES HIS CONNECTION TO SAURON.

-

"THE LORD OF THE RINGS: THE RETURN OF THE KING" MADE HISTORY AS THE SECOND FILM IN A TRILOGY TO RECEIVE BEST PICTURE NOMINATIONS AT BOTH THE ACADEMY AWARDS AND THE GOLDEN GLOBES, FOLLOWING "THE GODFATHER PART III" IN 1990. IT ALSO STANDS AS THE ONLY THIRD FILM IN A TRILOGY TO WIN THE BEST PICTURE OSCAR.

JOHN NOBLE'S CHARACTER, DENETHOR, CARRIES A SWORD ON HIS BELT THROUGHOUT THE MOVIE. ALTHOUGH HE NEVER DRAWS IT, THE PROP DEPARTMENT CRAFTED A FULLY FUNCTIONAL SWORD THAT COULD BE UNSHEATHED, ENSURING NOBLE FELT JUST AS IMPORTANT AS THE REST OF THE CAST WHO UTILIZED THEIR WEAPONS.

-

LEGOLAS' DIALOGUE IN THE EXTENDED EDITION SCENE OF THE PATHS OF THE DEAD CLOSELY MIRRORS DIRECT QUOTES FROM THE BOOK, MAINTAINING A FAITHFUL CONNECTION TO J.R.R. TOLKIEN'S ORIGINAL TEXT.

-

WHILE COMPOSER HOWARD SHORE'S SCORE FOR "THE LORD OF THE RINGS" DEVIATED FROM HIS USUAL STYLE, DIRECTOR PETER JACKSON INSTRUCTED HIM TO APPROACH THE SHELOB'S LAIR SCENE AS IF SCORING A FILM FOR DAVID CRONENBERG. THIS DIRECTION AIMED TO CAPTURE A SIMILAR ATMOSPHERE TO CRONENBERG'S 1986 MOVIE "THE FLY" (LA MOSCA).

THE FIRST SHOT OF SAM'S ARM ENTERING THE
FRAME, HOLDING STING TOWARDS SHELOB, IS
ACTUALLY DIRECTOR PETER JACKSON'S ARM,
ADDING A PERSONAL TOUCH TO THE SCENE.

-

INITIALLY, ANDY SERKIS WAS NOT THE
FILMMAKERS' FIRST CHOICE TO PORTRAY THE
REAL SMEAGOL AT THE BEGINNING OF THE
MOVIE. HOWEVER, AS THEY EXPLORED OTHER
OPTIONS, THEY REALIZED THAT SERKIS
POSSESSED THE NATURAL TALENT REQUIRED FOR
THE ROLE, ULTIMATELY MAKING HIM THE
PERFECT CHOICE.

-

DURING THE "FALL OF SMEAGOL" SCENE, TWO DIGITAL TOUCH-UPS WERE NECESSARY. FIRSTLY, THOMAS ROBINS, PORTRAYING DEAGOL, ACCIDENTALLY BLINKED AFTER BEING STRANGLED, BUT THE SHOT WAS PREFERRED, SO THE WETA DIGITAL TEAM FROZE HIS EYES DIGITALLY. SECONDLY, ANDY SERKIS' LEGS APPEARED TOO MUSCULAR AND ATHLETIC IN THE SHOT WHERE SMEAGOL FALLS ON THE ROCKS, PROMPTING DIGITAL MODIFICATIONS TO CREATE A MORE FITTING APPEARANCE FOR THE CHARACTER.

-

DURING THE FILMING OF THE SCENE WHERE MERRY AND PIPPIN ENJOY THEIR PIPES AT ISENGARD, DOMINIC MONAGHAN, WHO PLAYED MERRY, HAD TO CONSUME A GLASS OF MILK BEFOREHAND TO PREVENT NAUSEA WHILE SMOKING THE PROP PIPE.

-

LAWRENCE MAKOARE SHOWCASED HIS VERSATILITY BY PORTRAYING BOTH THE WITCH-KING OF ANGMAR AND THE ORC GOTHMOG. THESE CHARACTERS HAVE A MEMORABLE EXCHANGE OF DIALOGUE, AND EOWYN ENGAGES IN COMBAT WITH BOTH OF THEM, INJURING GOTHMOG AND ULTIMATELY SLAYING THE WITCH-KING.

-

BRET MCKENZIE, KNOWN FOR HIS ROLE AS AN ELF, MADE A SILENT CAMEO IN "THE LORD OF THE RINGS: THE FELLOWSHIP OF THE RING." FANS WERE CAPTIVATED BY HIS ATTRACTIVE CHARACTER AND AFFECTIONATELY DUBBED HIM "FIGWIT," AN ACRONYM FOR "FRODO IS GREAT...WHO IS THAT?!?" DIRECTOR PETER JACKSON ACKNOWLEDGED MCKENZIE'S ONLINE FAME AND INVITED HIM BACK FOR THIS MOVIE AS ARWEN'S ESCORT, GRANTING HIM TWO SCRIPTED LINES OF DIALOGUE.

-

THE POIGNANT LAST WORDS SHARED BETWEEN ELROND AND ARAGORN, "I GIVE HOPE TO MEN" AND "I KEEP NONE FOR MYSELF," ARE DERIVED FROM APPENDIX A OF THE BOOK. THESE LINES REPRESENT THE FINAL WORDS SPOKEN BY ARAGORN'S MOTHER, GILRAEN, IN ELVISH (ONEN I-ESTEL EDAIN, U-CHEBIN ESTEL ANIM). ESTEL, MEANING HOPE, WAS ALSO ARAGORN'S NAME BEFORE HIS TRUE LINEAGE WAS REVEALED.

-

A FASCINATING BEHIND-THE-SCENES MOMENT OCCURRED WHEN VIGGO MORTENSEN, FULLY IMMERSED IN HIS ROLE AS ARAGORN, CONVERSED WITH DIRECTOR PETER JACKSON. JACKSON INADVERTENTLY REFERRED TO MORTENSEN AS "ARAGORN" FOR OVER HALF AN HOUR, A TESTAMENT TO MORTENSEN'S DEDICATION AND EMBODIMENT OF THE CHARACTER.

-

THE WITCH-KING OF ANGMAR UNDERWENT A
REDESIGN FROM THE ORIGINAL CONCEPT, WHICH
FEATURED A HELMET RESEMBLING A SPIKED
BUCKET. TEST FOOTAGE REVEALED SIMILARITIES
TO SAURON'S HELMET FROM "THE LORD OF THE
RINGS: THE FELLOWSHIP OF THE RING,"
PROMPTING PRODUCERS TO PAY HOMAGE TO THE
RINGWRAITH DESIGNS INSTEAD. ADDITIONALLY,
THE WITCH-KING'S FLAIL WAS INITIALLY
ENLARGED UPON JACKSON'S REQUEST, BUT IT
EVENTUALLY BECAME TOO LARGE AND HEAVY
FOR PRACTICAL USE IN FIGHT SCENES, LEADING
TO ITS REPLACEMENT WITH A DIGITAL VERSION.

-

DURING THE SCENE WHERE THE HOBBITS RETURN
TO HOBBITON, SEVERAL CHALLENGES AROSE FOR
THE ACTORS. ELIJAH WOOD STRUGGLED TO
CONTROL HIS PONY, SEAN ASTIN EXPERIENCED
ALLERGIES TO THE PONIES, AND DOMINIC
MONAGHAN'S MOOD WAS AFFECTED BY
TECHNICAL ASPECTS SURROUNDING THE SCENE.
HOWEVER, BILLY BOYD FOUND THE SITUATION
AMUSING AND COULDN'T HELP BUT LAUGH
THROUGHOUT THE SHOOT.

-

TO ACHIEVE THE DESIRED PERSPECTIVE IN THE SCENE WHERE DENETHOR FORCEFULLY DRAGS AND THROWS OUT PIPPIN FROM THE BURIAL CHAMBER, BILLY BOYD'S DOUBLE WAS EMPLOYED FOR THE PHYSICAL ACTIONS. DURING THE SEQUENCE, THE DOUBLE ACCIDENTALLY STRUCK BOYD IN THE BACK, CAUSING HIM TO POP UP UNEXPECTEDLY.

-

IN AN INTERESTING COLLABORATION, LAWRENCE MAKOARE PORTRAYED THE WITCH-KING OF ANGMAR PHYSICALLY, BUT THE CHARACTER'S VOICE WAS PERFORMED BY ANDY SERKIS, KNOWN FOR HIS ROLE AS GOLLUM. THIS COMBINATION OF TALENTS CONTRIBUTED TO THE EERIE PRESENCE AND CHARACTERIZATION OF THE WITCH-KING.

-

THE CONFRONTATION BETWEEN SARUMAN AND GANDALF, DERIVED FROM THE SECOND BOOK IN THE SERIES, WAS FILMED BUT DID NOT MAKE THE FINAL CUT DUE TO CONSIDERATIONS OF LENGTH AND PACING. HOWEVER, THIS SCENE IS INCLUDED IN THE DVD RELEASE, ALLOWING VIEWERS TO EXPERIENCE THE POWERFUL ENCOUNTER BETWEEN THE TWO ICONIC CHARACTERS.

-

THE TRILOGY'S SUCCESS ALLOWED NEW LINE CINEMA TO CLAIM TAX BREAKS THAT AMOUNTED TO TEN TIMES THE ANNUAL BUDGET OF THE NEW ZEALAND FILM COMMISSION, WHICH SUPPORTS LOCAL FILMMAKING. THIS FINANCIAL ADVANTAGE DEMONSTRATED THE SIGNIFICANT IMPACT THE PRODUCTION HAD ON THE COUNTRY'S ECONOMY.

-

MIRANDA OTTO, WHO PORTRAYED EOWYN, UNDERWENT MULTIPLE FITTINGS TO FIND A HELMET DESIGN THAT CONCEALED HER FACE WHILE STILL REVEALING ENOUGH TO ENSURE AUDIENCE RECOGNITION. THE METICULOUS PROCESS AIMED TO STRIKE A BALANCE BETWEEN DISGUISE AND FAMILIARITY FOR THE CHARACTER.

-

THE WETA VISUAL EFFECTS TEAM FACED A FORMIDABLE CHALLENGE WHEN CREATING THE CHARACTER OF SHELOB, PARTLY DUE TO THE IMPRESSIVE PORTRAYAL OF A GIANT SPIDER IN "HARRY POTTER AND THE CHAMBER OF SECRETS" (2002). THE TEAM HAD TO SURPASS THE STANDARD SET BY THEIR PREVIOUS ARACHNID CREATION WHILE ADDING THEIR OWN UNIQUE TOUCH.

-

ANDY SERKIS, RENOWNED FOR HIS PORTRAYAL OF GOLLUM, COMPLETED HIS FINAL DAY OF FILMING JUST A FEW WEEKS BEFORE THE THEATRICAL RELEASE. IN A CASUAL SETTING, THEY FILMED GOLLUM'S FACIAL REACTION AS HE REALIZES FRODO'S INTENTION TO DESTROY THE RING. THE RESULTING FOOTAGE WAS THEN SHARED WITH WETA DIGITAL, ALLOWING THE ANIMATORS TO REPLICATE THE SHOT WITH THE CGI CHARACTER.

-

THE MINAS TIRITH SET, WHICH SERVED AS THE GRAND CAPITAL CITY OF GONDOR, WAS CONSTRUCTED ON THE SAME LOCATION USED FOR HELM'S DEEP. ONCE THE HELM'S DEEP SCENES WERE FILMED, THE SET WAS TRANSFORMED AND BUILT UPON TO CREATE THE MAJESTIC MINAS TIRITH, DEMONSTRATING THE RESOURCEFULNESS OF THE PRODUCTION TEAM.

-

ORLANDO BLOOM'S MEMORABLE HEROIC SCENE ATOP THE MÛMAKIL, THE MASSIVE ELEPHANT-LIKE CREATURES, WAS EFFICIENTLY SHOT IN JUST A SINGLE DAY. THE ACTOR DELIVERED HIS PERFORMANCE WHILE PERCHED ATOP A PILE OF SANDBAGS, SKILLFULLY PORTRAYING LEGOLAS IN ACTION.

-

ORIGINALLY, SCENES WERE FILMED INVOLVING ARAGORN ENGAGING IN A PHYSICAL CONFRONTATION WITH A PHYSICAL MANIFESTATION OF SAURON OUTSIDE THE BLACK GATE. SAURON WOULD HAVE APPEARED EVEN TALLER THAN THE VERSION SEEN AT THE BEGINNING OF "THE FELLOWSHIP OF THE RING." HOWEVER, UPON REVIEWING THE FOOTAGE, IT WAS DECIDED THAT INCLUDING THIS SCENE WOULD DEVIATE FROM J.R.R. TOLKIEN'S ORIGINAL IDEAS AND DISTRACT FROM THE CLIMACTIC FOCUS ON FRODO AND SAM'S JOURNEY. CERTAIN ELEMENTS FROM THE FIGHT WERE REPURPOSED: ARAGORN'S INITIAL CONFRONTATION WITH AN IMAGE OF SAURON SHIFTED TO HIM GAZING AT THE EYE OF SAURON ATOP THE TOWER OF BARAD-DÛR. FURTHERMORE, HIS CHARGE TOWARD THE BLACK GATE CULMINATED IN A HEATED SWORD FIGHT WITH THE REAL SAURON, PORTRAYED BY A STUNTMAN WITH A DIGITAL TROLL IMPOSED OVER HIM.

-

"THE LORD OF THE RINGS: THE RETURN OF THE KING" MADE HISTORY AS THE FIRST FANTASY FILM TO WIN THE PRESTIGIOUS ACADEMY AWARD FOR BEST PICTURE. THIS REMARKABLE ACHIEVEMENT SOLIDIFIED THE TRILOGY'S CRITICAL ACCLAIM AND RECOGNITION IN THE FILM INDUSTRY.

-

IN FEBRUARY 2004, THE MOVIE BECAME THE SECOND FILM EVER TO SURPASS THE REMARKABLE MILESTONE OF EARNING OVER $1 BILLION IN WORLDWIDE BOX OFFICE REVENUE. THE FIRST FILM TO ACHIEVE THIS FEAT WAS "TITANIC" IN 1997, SHOWCASING THE IMMENSE POPULARITY AND COMMERCIAL SUCCESS OF "THE LORD OF THE RINGS: THE RETURN OF THE KING."

-

ARAGORN'S POWERFUL SPEECH TO THE TROOPS, BEGINNING WITH THE ICONIC LINE "A DAY MAY COME WHEN THE COURAGE OF MEN FAILS," BEARS A STRIKING RESEMBLANCE TO THE 45TH STANZA OF THE OLD NORSE POEM VOLUSPÅ, WHICH DESCRIBES RAGNAROK, THE APOCALYPSE. THE SIMILARITIES IN THEME AND LANGUAGE HIGHLIGHT THE INFLUENCE OF NORSE MYTHOLOGY ON J.R.R. TOLKIEN'S CREATION. FURTHERMORE, THE SAME POEM ALSO INSPIRED SEVERAL OF THE DWARVES' NAMES IN TOLKIEN'S WORLD, DEMONSTRATING THE AUTHOR'S DEEP APPRECIATION FOR MYTHOLOGICAL SOURCES.

-

COMPOSER HOWARD SHORE AND CONDUCTOR LUDWIG WICKI HAVE COLLABORATED SINCE 2007 TO BRING THE ENCHANTING SCORE OF "THE LORD OF THE RINGS" MOVIES TO THE CONCERT HALL. THE COMPLETE SYMPHONY ORCHESTRA AND CHORUS PERFORM THE SCORE LIVE WHILE SYNCHRONIZED WITH THE FILMS, OFFERING AUDIENCES A CAPTIVATING AND IMMERSIVE MUSICAL EXPERIENCE.

-

DURING THE EDITING PROCESS OF THE TRILOGY, JOHN GILBERT WORKED ON "THE FELLOWSHIP OF THE RING," MICHAEL HORTON ON "THE TWO TOWERS," AND JAMIE SELKIRK HAD THE RESPONSIBILITY OF EDITING THE FINAL CHAPTER, "THE RETURN OF THE KING." DIRECTOR PETER JACKSON SPECIFICALLY CHOSE SELKIRK FOR THIS CRUCIAL TASK, CONFIDENT IN HIS ABILITY TO MAINTAIN FOCUS ON THE CLIMACTIC CONCLUSION OF THE EPIC SAGA.

-

THE STEPS OF CIRITH UNGOL, A CHALLENGING SET WHERE SEAN ASTIN, ELIJAH WOOD, AND ANDY SERKIS FILMED CRUCIAL SCENES, WERE CRAFTED FROM POLYSTYRENE. HOWEVER, DUE TO THEIR STEEP AND DELICATE NATURE, THE STEPS OCCASIONALLY BROKE. MOREOVER, THE STEPS WERE SPRAYED WITH WATER, CAUSING ASTIN AND WOOD, WEARING THEIR HOBBIT FEET, TO OCCASIONALLY GET STUCK AND REQUIRE ASSISTANCE TO FREE THEMSELVES.

-

DOMINIC MONAGHAN, WHO PORTRAYED MERRY, HAD AN UNUSUAL ALLERGIC REACTION TO THE ELVEN CLOAKS WORN BY THE FELLOWSHIP. DIRECTOR PETER JACKSON WOULD PLAYFULLY INQUIRE IF MONAGHAN WAS READY TO FILM, JOKINGLY REFERENCING THE CLOAK AND ENSURING EVERYTHING WAS IN ORDER BEFORE SHOOTING COMMENCED.

-

IN THE SCENE WHERE FRODO IS TRAPPED IN SHELOB'S WEB AND TAUNTED BY GOLLUM, ELIJAH WOOD WAS ACTUALLY SUSPENDED ON A HARNESS WITH BUNGEE CORDS ATTACHED TO HIS WRISTS AND ANKLES. HE HUMOROUSLY QUIPS IN THE COMMENTARY THAT HIS PRESENCE IN THE WEB WAS NOT SOLELY DUE TO THE STRENGTH OF THE SPIDER'S CREATION.

-

ON ELIJAH WOOD'S FINAL DAY OF FILMING, AN EMOTIONAL ATMOSPHERE ENVELOPED THE SET AS EACH ACTOR BID FAREWELL TO THEIR CHARACTERS. WOOD'S DEPARTURE WAS PARTICULARLY POIGNANT, AND DIRECTOR PETER JACKSON REPEATEDLY SHOT FRODO'S LINE, "THERE'S ROOM FOR A LITTLE MORE," RELUCTANT TO BRING AN END TO THE EXTRAORDINARY JOURNEY. WHEN THE SCENE WAS FINALLY WRAPPED, THE ROOM ERUPTED IN APPLAUSE, AND JACKSON, DEEPLY MOVED, EMBRACED WOOD, EXPRESSING HIS HEARTFELT GRATITUDE.

-

IN THE CROWD SHOT DURING ARAGORN'S ASCENSION SCENE, KEEN-EYED VIEWERS CAN SPOT A BLUE BANNER FEATURING THE SILVER SWAN OF DOL AMROTH BEING WAVED. ALTHOUGH THE CHARACTER OF PRINCE IMRAHIL OF DOL AMROTH DOES NOT PLAY A PROMINENT ROLE IN THE FILM, HE IS RESPONSIBLE FOR DISCOVERING EOWYN'S SURVIVAL AFTER HER CONFRONTATION WITH THE WITCH-KING.

-

THE MODEL FOR THE MENACING SPIDER SHELOB WAS BASED ON THE APPEARANCE OF A NEW ZEALAND FUNNEL WEB SPIDER. THIS REAL-LIFE INSPIRATION HELPED BRING AN AUTHENTIC AND UNSETTLING QUALITY TO THE CHARACTER'S DESIGN.

-

DIRECTOR PETER JACKSON INTENTIONALLY AVOIDED SHOWING FRODO'S LEFT HAND IN LATER SCENES FOLLOWING THE MORDOR SEQUENCES. THIS DELIBERATE CHOICE AIMED TO PREVENT ANY DISCREPANCIES CONCERNING THE POSITIONING OF THE WOUND ON FRODO'S INDEX FINGER. THE HAND IS ONLY SEEN TWICE: WHEN THE FELLOWSHIP IS REUNITED (WITH THE HAND BANDAGED) AND WHEN FRODO WRITES THE FINAL PAGES OF THE RED BOOK BEFORE ADDING THE TITLE.

-

THE HAUNTING TRANSFORMATION OF SMÉAGOL
INTO GOLLUM DURING THE OPENING FLASHBACK
SCENE DREW SIGNIFICANT INSPIRATION FROM
THE FINAL TRANSFORMATION OF SETH BRUNDLE
INTO BRUNDLEFLY IN THE FILM "THE FLY" (1986).
THIS PARALLEL SERVED AS A CREATIVE
INFLUENCE IN DEPICTING GOLLUM'S DRAMATIC
PHYSICAL AND PSYCHOLOGICAL
METAMORPHOSIS.

-

ON THE EXTENDED EDITION DVD, THERE ARE
HIDDEN EASTER EGGS TO DISCOVER. ON DISC
ONE, NAVIGATE TO THE SCENE SELECTION
MENU'S LAST PAGE AND PRESS DOWN UNTIL A
RING ICON APPEARS NEXT TO THE "NEW SCENE"
PHRASE. THIS REVEALS A SATELLITE "INTERVIEW"
OF ELIJAH WOOD CONDUCTED BY DOMINIC
MONAGHAN IN A GERMAN ACCENT. SIMILARLY,
ON DISC TWO, FOLLOW THE SAME STEPS TO
UNCOVER AN MTV SKIT FEATURING BEN STILLER
AND VINCE VAUGHN PITCHING THE LORD OF THE
RINGS SEQUELS TO SIR PETER JACKSON.

-

TO CAPTURE INTENSE SHOTS DURING THE BATTLE ON THE PELENNOR FIELDS, DIRECTOR OF PHOTOGRAPHY ANDREW LESNIE IMMERSED HIMSELF IN THE ACTION BY DONNING POLO ARMOR AND VENTURING INTO THE MIDST OF THE BATTLE. THIS HANDS-ON APPROACH ALLOWED HIM TO CAPTURE DYNAMIC AND IMMERSIVE FOOTAGE FOR THE FILM.

-

THE CONVERSATION BETWEEN ARAGORN AND EOWYN BEFORE ARAGORN DEPARTS ON THE PATHS OF THE DEAD UNDERWENT CHANGES FROM THE BOOK TO THE FILM ADAPTATION. IN THE BOOK, THIS INTERACTION IS THEIR FIRST ENCOUNTER AND A LENGTHIER SCENE. IT INVOLVES EOWYN PRESENTING ARAGORN WITH A GOBLET OF MEAD, AND THEIR DISCUSSION DELVES INTO EOWYN'S FEAR OF BEING TRAPPED AND HER ADMIRATION FOR ARAGORN'S FOLLOWERS. SINCE THE CHARACTERS HAD MET EARLIER IN THE MOVIES, THESE STORY ELEMENTS WERE INCORPORATED INTO EARLIER EXCHANGES BETWEEN THEM IN THIS FILM AND THE TWO TOWERS.

-

THE BEACON SYSTEM DEPICTED IN THE FILM DRAWS INSPIRATION FROM A REAL SYSTEM UTILIZED BY THE BYZANTINE EMPIRE DURING THE ARAB-BYZANTINE WARS. THE BYZANTINES EMPLOYED BEACON FIRES ALONG THEIR BORDERS TO QUICKLY ALERT CONSTANTINOPLE, THEIR CAPITAL CITY, OF POTENTIAL ATTACKS. THIS SYSTEM ALLOWED THEM TO RECEIVE TIMELY INFORMATION, OFTEN FASTER THAN A RIDER COULD ARRIVE. THE BEACON SYSTEM SHOWCASED IN THE MOVIE, SIMILAR TO MINAS TIRITH, FEATURED LAYERS OF WALLS, ENSURING THE RULERS WOULD LEARN OF IMPENDING ATTACKS WITHIN AN HOUR. NOTABLY, DURING THE 9TH CENTURY, THE CHINESE ALSO EMPLOYED A COMPARABLE SYSTEM, UTILIZING BONFIRES COVERED WITH WOLF DUNG THAT WOULD RISE TO HIGH ALTITUDES WITHOUT DISSIPATING.

-

A SCENE DEPICTING EOWYN (MIRANDA OTTO) CHANGING INTO THE ARMOR OF A ROHAN WARRIOR WAS FILMED BUT ULTIMATELY OMITTED FROM THE FINAL MOVIE. THIS SEQUENCE SHOWCASED EOWYN SHEDDING HER REGULAR CLOTHES AND PREPARING HERSELF FOR BATTLE, EMPHASIZING HER TRANSFORMATION AND RESOLVE.

-

THE COMBINED RUNNING TIME OF THE LORD OF THE RINGS TRILOGY AMOUNTS TO APPROXIMATELY TWELVE HOURS, PROVIDING AUDIENCES WITH AN EPIC AND IMMERSIVE CINEMATIC EXPERIENCE THAT SPANS THE ENTIRETY OF J.R.R. TOLKIEN'S ENCHANTING WORLD.

-

ANDY SERKIS'S FIRST SCENE AS GOLLUM TOOK PLACE ATOP MOUNT DOOM NEAR THE CRACKS OF DOOM. HIS FINAL SCENE INVOLVED THE INTENSE FIGHT BETWEEN GOLLUM AND FRODO, CULMINATING IN THEIR FALL OFF THE LEDGE. SERKIS'S PORTRAYAL OF GOLLUM EVOLVED THROUGHOUT THE TRILOGY, MARKING HIS JOURNEY FROM THE TREACHEROUS GUIDE TO FRODO'S TORMENTOR.

-

THE FILM SHATTERED THE INTERNATIONAL BOX-OFFICE RECORD FOR THE LARGEST OPENING WEEKEND, AMASSING NEARLY $250 MILLION IN REVENUE. THIS UNPRECEDENTED SUCCESS SOLIDIFIED THE IMMENSE POPULARITY AND APPEAL OF THE LORD OF THE RINGS FRANCHISE.

-

THE VISUAL EFFECTS IN EACH INSTALLMENT OF THE LORD OF THE RINGS TRILOGY PROGRESSIVELY INCREASED. "THE FELLOWSHIP OF THE RING" CONTAINED 540 COMPUTER-GENERATED EFFECTS, "THE TWO TOWERS" FEATURED 799, AND THIS FILM, "THE RETURN OF THE KING," BOASTED AN IMPRESSIVE 1,487 VISUAL EFFECTS SHOTS. THE CONTINUOUS ADVANCEMENT IN TECHNOLOGY AND THE FILMMAKERS' DEDICATION TO CREATING IMMERSIVE VISUAL LANDSCAPES CONTRIBUTED TO THE TRILOGY'S VISUAL SPLENDOR.

-

IN THE ORIGINAL NOVEL OF THE LORD OF THE RINGS, THE DEFORMED ORC LEADER GOTHMOG IS MENTIONED ONLY ONCE AS THE LIEUTENANT OF MORGUL, WITH NO SPECIFIC DETAILS ABOUT HIS RACE. THE FILMMAKERS MADE THE CREATIVE DECISION TO PORTRAY HIM AS AN ORC IN THE MOVIE ADAPTATION. INTERESTINGLY, THE NAME GOTHMOG IS ALSO USED FOR THE LEADER OF THE BALROGS IN MORGOTH'S ARMY IN J.R.R. TOLKIEN'S "THE SILMARILLION," WHICH TAKES PLACE MILLENNIA BEFORE THE EVENTS IN THE LORD OF THE RINGS.

\-

THROUGHOUT THE TRILOGY, THE NAMES OF VARIOUS LOCATIONS HAVE TRANSLATIONS FROM THE SINDARIN LANGUAGE. FOR EXAMPLE, RIVENDELL/IMLADRIS TRANSLATES TO "ELVEN OUTPOST" OR "DEEP VALLEY OF THE CLEFT," LOTHLÓRIEN MEANS "DREAM FLOWER," ISENGARD SIGNIFIES "IRON FORTRESS," CARADHRAS REPRESENTS "RED HORN," AND ANDUIN REFERS TO THE "LONG RIVER." OTHER EXAMPLES INCLUDE ARGONATH MEANING "TWO NOBLE STONES," EMYN MUIL BEING "THE DREAR HILLS," FANGORN REPRESENTING "TREEBEARD," ROHAN SIGNIFYING THE "HORSE COUNTRY," GONDOR BEING THE "LAND OF STONE," OSGILIATH REFERRING TO THE "CITADEL OF THE HOST OF STARS," MINAS TIRITH MEANING THE "TOWER OF WATCH," MINAS MORGUL REPRESENTING THE "TOWER OF DARK SORCERY," MORIA SIGNIFYING THE "BLACK CHASM," CIRITH UNGOL BEING THE "PASS OF THE SPIDER," AND MORDOR REFERRING TO THE "BLACK LAND." THESE CAREFULLY CHOSEN NAMES ADD DEPTH AND MEANING TO THE WORLD OF MIDDLE-EARTH.

\-

THE MOVIE ACHIEVED A REMARKABLE FEAT BY TYING WITH "BEN-HUR" (1959) AND "TITANIC" (1997) FOR THE RECORD OF WINNING THE MOST OSCARS IN A SINGLE YEAR, WITH A TOTAL OF ELEVEN ACADEMY AWARDS. HOWEVER, IT IS THE ONLY FILM AMONG THE THREE TO HAVE ALSO WON THE OSCAR FOR BEST ADAPTED SCREENPLAY. THIS RECOGNITION UNDERSCORES THE EXCEPTIONAL QUALITY AND SUCCESS OF THE LORD OF THE RINGS: THE RETURN OF THE KING.

-

IN THE EXTENDED DVD EXTRAS, SIR PETER JACKSON REVEALS THE INSPIRATION BEHIND THE APPEARANCE OF GOTHMOG, THE LEADER OF THE ORCS DURING THE SIEGE OF GONDOR. THE DESIGN OF GOTHMOG'S HEAD WAS PARTIALLY DERIVED FROM THE HEAD OF JOSEPH "JOHN" MERRICK, FAMOUSLY KNOWN AS "THE ELEPHANT MAN." ADDITIONALLY, THE ALIEN LEADER FROM JACKSON'S EARLIER FILM, "BAD TASTE" (1987), ALSO INFLUENCED GOTHMOG'S CHARACTER DESIGN. THESE REFERENCES HIGHLIGHT THE DIRECTOR'S ARTISTIC CHOICES AND ATTENTION TO DETAIL.

THE EXTENDED EDITION DVD VERSION INCLUDES A SCENE FEATURING THE "CORSAIRS OF UMBAR" BEING ATTACKED BY THE ARMY OF THE DEAD. THIS SEQUENCE INCLUDES SEVERAL CAMEOS BY INDIVIDUALS INVOLVED IN THE FILMMAKING PROCESS. SIR PETER JACKSON HIMSELF APPEARS AND GETS HIT BY LEGOLAS'S ARROW, PERFORMING MULTIPLE TAKES WITHOUT ANY PADDING. CO-PRODUCER RICK PORRAS IS SEEN WITH A "LOOK OF HORROR" AS THE GHOSTLY HORDE ATTACKS. OTHER RECOGNIZABLE FIGURES IN THE SCENE INCLUDE WETA SUPERVISOR SIR RICHARD TAYLOR, PROSTHETICS SUPERVISOR GINO ACEVEDO, AND DIRECTOR OF PHOTOGRAPHY ANDREW LESNIE. THESE CAMEOS ADD A TOUCH OF FUN AND BEHIND-THE-SCENES CAMARADERIE TO THE FILM.

-

REMARKABLY, THIS IS THE SECOND FILM
FEATURING BERNARD HILL, WHO PORTRAYS KING
THEODEN, TO WIN ELEVEN ACADEMY AWARDS.
THE FIRST FILM WAS "TITANIC" (1997), WHERE
HILL PLAYED CAPTAIN EDWARD SMITH. HILL'S
INVOLVEMENT IN BOTH FILMS SPEAKS TO HIS
TALENT AND CONTRIBUTIONS TO THESE
CRITICALLY ACCLAIMED PRODUCTIONS.

-

DURING THE SCENE WHERE FARAMIR AND HIS
SOLDIERS DEPART FROM MINAS TIRITH, THEY ARE
SEEN RIDING DOWNHILL. HOWEVER, THE
SMOOTH BRICK-PAVED STREETS POSED A
CHALLENGE AS THE HORSES' STEEL HORSESHOES
PROVED TO BE TOO SLIPPERY. TO ENSURE SAFETY
AND STABILITY, ALL THE HORSES WERE RE-SHOD
WITH RUBBER HORSESHOES, ALLOWING FOR A
SMOOTHER AND MORE CONTROLLED RIDE.

-

INTERESTINGLY, JOHN RHYS-DAVIES, THE ACTOR WHO PORTRAYED GIMLI, ORIGINALLY AUDITIONED FOR THE ROLE OF DENETHOR. WHILE ULTIMATELY LANDING THE ICONIC ROLE OF THE DWARF WARRIOR, RHYS-DAVIES INITIALLY TRIED OUT FOR A DIFFERENT CHARACTER IN THE LORD OF THE RINGS.

-

DIRECTOR SIR PETER JACKSON WAS DETERMINED TO HAVE THE WORLD PREMIERE OF THIS MOVIE IN HIS HOME COUNTRY OF NEW ZEALAND, WHERE THE ENTIRE TRILOGY HAD BEEN FILMED. DURING PROMOTIONAL TOURS FOR THE PREVIOUS FILM, JACKSON HINTED AT A SPECIAL SURPRISE FOR NEW ZEALAND FANS, ESSENTIALLY FORCING PRODUCER MARK ORDESKY TO PROMISE THAT WELLINGTON WOULD HOST THE WORLD PREMIERE. THIS DECISION FULFILLED JACKSON'S DESIRE TO CELEBRATE THE CULMINATION OF THE TRILOGY IN THE PLACE IT WAS BROUGHT TO LIFE.

-

THE ORIGINAL STORYBOARDS FOR THE
DESTRUCTION OF BARAD-DÛR, THE DARK TOWER,
DEPICTED A VOLCANIC FISSURE EMERGING
BETWEEN MOUNT DOOM AND THE TOWER ITSELF.
IN THIS VERSION, LAVA WOULD ERUPT INTO THE
TOWER, MELTING IT FROM WITHIN. HOWEVER, DUE
TO THE DEMANDING POST-PRODUCTION
SCHEDULE, THE SEQUENCE WAS SIMPLIFIED, AND
THE FINAL VERSION OF THE SCENE SHOWCASED
IN THE FILM TOOK A DIFFERENT APPROACH.

-

GOLLUM, THE TORMENTED CREATURE OBSESSED
WITH THE ONE RING, UTTERS THE WORD
"PRECIOUS" A TOTAL OF SEVENTEEN TIMES IN
THIS MOVIE. THIS REPETITION EMPHASIZES HIS
FIXATION ON THE RING AND HIS INTERNAL
STRUGGLE FOR CONTROL.

-

ACCORDING TO THE LONDON DAILY MAIL, THE STARS OF THE LORD OF THE RINGS TRILOGY RECEIVED BONUSES IN ADDITION TO THEIR SALARIES BASED ON THEIR INVOLVEMENT IN THE TRILOGY. ACTORS SUCH AS ELIJAH WOOD, SEAN ASTIN, BILLY BOYD, AND DOMINIC MONAGHAN RECEIVED BONUSES RANGING FROM $430,000 TO $560,000 PER MOVIE. BERNARD HILL AND SIR IAN MCKELLEN EARNED $312,000 PER MOVIE, WHILE LIV TYLER'S BONUS WAS SLIGHTLY LOWER.

-

LAWRENCE MAKOARE, THE ACTOR WEARING THE GOTHMOG MAKEUP, EARNED THE NICKNAME "PIMPLEHEAD" FROM EXTRAS WHO WERE UNAWARE OF HIS ACTUAL NAME. THIS AMUSING ANECDOTE HIGHLIGHTS THE INFORMAL AND LIGHTHEARTED ATMOSPHERE ON SET, WHERE CAST AND CREW OFTEN DEVELOPED PLAYFUL NICKNAMES AND INSIDE JOKES.

-

DAVID WENHAM, THE ACTOR WHO PORTRAYED FARAMIR, BEGAN HIS FILMING JOURNEY WITH THE HOUSE OF THE HEALING SEQUENCE. IT MARKED HIS FIRST DAY ON SET, IMMERSING HIM IN THE WORLD OF THE LORD OF THE RINGS AND INTRODUCING HIM TO THE FILMING PROCESS.

-

THE EERIE SOUNDS OF THE ORCS WERE ACHIEVED BY INCORPORATING RECORDINGS OF ELEPHANT SEAL PUPS FROM THE MARINE MAMMAL CENTER IN SAUSALITO, CALIFORNIA. THIS ORGANIZATION SERVES AS A HOSPITAL FOR SICK AND INJURED MARINE MAMMALS, INCLUDING SEALS, SEA LIONS, WHALES, AND DOLPHINS. BY UTILIZING THESE RECORDINGS, THE FILMMAKERS ADDED A DISTINCT AND OTHERWORLDLY QUALITY TO THE ORCS' VOCALIZATIONS.

-

BRUCE SPENCE PORTRAYS THE CHARACTER KNOWN AS THE MOUTH OF SAURON IN THE EXTENDED EDITION DVD. TO EMPHASIZE HIS POSITION AS A SERVANT OF SAURON AND ENHANCE HIS INHUMAN APPEARANCE, SPENCE'S REAL MOUTH WAS DIGITALLY ENLARGED. THIS ALTERATION NOT ONLY HIGHLIGHTED THE CHARACTER'S SIGNIFICANCE BUT ALSO CONTRIBUTED TO HIS MENACING PRESENCE.

-

DURING A CONVERSATION WITH GANDALF, TREEBEARD REFERS TO THE WIZARD AS "YOUNG MASTER GANDALF," IMPLYING THAT TREEBEARD IS SIGNIFICANTLY OLDER THAN GANDALF. IN THE PREVIOUS FILM, GANDALF MENTIONS HAVING LIVED FOR "THREE HUNDRED LIFETIMES." CONSIDERING DIFFERENT INTERPRETATIONS OF LIFETIMES, WHETHER AS GENERATIONS OR CUMULATIVE LIFESPANS, GANDALF'S AGE RANGES FROM 6,000 TO 12,000 YEARS. THIS REVELATION ESTABLISHES TREEBEARD AS AN INCREDIBLY ANCIENT BEING.

-

THE FINAL SCENE FILMED DURING PRINCIPAL PHOTOGRAPHY DEPICTED GONDORIAN SOLDIERS DRESSING ARAGORN IN HIS REGAL ARMOR BEFORE HIS CORONATION. INTERESTINGLY, THE SOLDIERS IN THIS SCENE WERE PORTRAYED BY INDIVIDUALS FROM THE WARDROBE DEPARTMENT. ALTHOUGH THE SCENE WAS ULTIMATELY CUT FROM THE FINAL VERSION OF THE FILM, BEHIND-THE-SCENES FOOTAGE OF ITS PRODUCTION CAN BE FOUND IN THE EXTENDED EDITION DVD EXTRAS.

-

THE APPEARANCE OF GOTHMOG, THE DEFORMED ORC LEADER, DREW INSPIRATION FROM HARVEY WEINSTEIN. THIS DECISION STEMMED FROM WEINSTEIN'S INITIAL DESIRE TO CONDENSE THE TRILOGY INTO A SINGLE FILM DURING THE NEGOTIATION STAGE WITH MIRAMAX. ULTIMATELY, A DEAL WAS NOT REACHED, AND NEW LINE CINEMA STEPPED IN TO PRESERVE THE EPIC SAGA. THE RESEMBLANCE OF GOTHMOG'S CHARACTER DESIGN TO WEINSTEIN'S SERVED AS A SUBTLE NOD TO THIS SIGNIFICANT TURNING POINT IN THE PRODUCTION HISTORY.

-

THE LORD OF THE RINGS TRILOGY HOLDS THE
DISTINCTION OF BEING THE ONLY TRILOGY IN
WHICH ALL THREE MOVIES WERE NOMINATED
FOR THE "TOP 100 GREATEST FILMS OF ALL TIME"
BY THE AMERICAN FILM INSTITUTE. THIS
RECOGNITION REFLECTS THE ENDURING IMPACT
AND ACCLAIM GARNERED BY EACH INSTALLMENT,
SOLIDIFYING THE TRILOGY'S STATUS AS A
CINEMATIC MASTERPIECE.

-

THE 2011 BLU-RAY BONUS MATERIAL INCLUDES
SCENES FROM THE BOOK THAT WERE NOT
INCLUDED IN THE THEATRICAL RELEASE. ONE
SUCH SCENE SHOWCASES GOBLINS ATTACKING
THE FELLOWSHIP SHORTLY AFTER THEIR
DEPARTURE FROM RIVENDELL. THESE BONUS
FEATURES PROVIDE FANS WITH ADDITIONAL
GLIMPSES INTO THE RICH WORLD OF THE LORD
OF THE RINGS.

-

JOHN HOWE, A MEMBER OF THE PRODUCTION
TEAM, PLAYFULLY EXPRESSED HIS DESIRE TO
BRING HOME THE TWIN WATCHERS STATUES FROM

THE MINAS MORGUL SET. HIS HUMOROUS INTENTION WAS TO UTILIZE THESE STATUES TO DETER SOLICITORS FROM APPROACHING HIS HOUSE, ADDING A TOUCH OF MIDDLE-EARTH'S EERIE AMBIANCE TO HIS EVERYDAY LIFE.

-

THERE IS A WIDESPREAD MISCONCEPTION REGARDING THE FELL BEASTS, OFTEN INCORRECTLY REFERRED TO AS NAZGÛL. THIS MISUNDERSTANDING MAY HAVE STEMMED FROM VIDEO GAMES THAT COMBINED THE FELL BEAST AND RINGWRAITH AS A SINGLE UNIT REFERRED TO AS NAZGÛL. ADDITIONALLY, A LINE SPOKEN BY THE WITCH-KING OF ANGMAR IN THIS MOVIE, "DO NOT COME BETWEEN THE NAZGÛL AND HIS PREY," MIGHT HAVE CONTRIBUTED TO THE CONFUSION. HOWEVER, IT IS WORTH NOTING THAT THE WITCH-KING WAS REFERRING TO HIMSELF, AND THE NAZGÛL ACTUALLY REPRESENT THE RINGWRAITHS, WHILE THE FELL BEASTS ARE THEIR FORMIDABLE WINGED MOUNTS.

-

IN THE EXTENDED EDITION OF THE FILM, THERE IS A POIGNANT SCENE WHERE SAM REASSURES FRODO BY SAYING, "THERE'S LIGHT AND BEAUTY UP THERE THAT NO SHADOW CAN TOUCH." THE STAR SAM SEES HOLDS DEEPER SIGNIFICANCE— IT IS THE STAR OF EARENDIL, ALSO KNOWN AS THE EVENSTAR, WHICH IS THE NAMESAKE OF ARWEN. IN MIDDLE-EARTH MYTHOLOGY, THE STAR OF EARENDIL REPRESENTS VENUS AND IS ASSOCIATED WITH A HALF-ELF (ARWEN'S GRANDFATHER) ABOARD A FLYING SHIP, BEARING ONE OF THE THREE SILMARILS. THESE SILMARILS CONTAIN THE ANCIENT LIGHT OF THE TWO TREES, PREDATING THE SUN AND MOON. NOTABLY, THE STAR OF EARENDIL PLAYED A ROLE IN GALADRIEL'S PHIAL, THE SOURCE OF ITS RADIANT LIGHT.

-

THE DIGITAL ALTERATION OF THE MOUTH OF
SAURON'S MOUTH, CAUSING IT TO DECAY AND
BLEED, WAS A POST-PRODUCTION DECISION.
INITIALLY, THE IDEA OF TURNING THE MOUTH
SIDEWAYS TO APPEAR VERTICAL ON THE FACE
WAS REJECTED BY DIRECTOR PETER JACKSON.
INSTEAD, THE DESIGN TEAM OPTED TO ENLARGE
THE MOUTH DIGITALLY, MAKING IT TWICE ITS
ORIGINAL SIZE. THE ORIGINAL CONCEPT FOR THE
MOUTH OF SAURON'S COSTUME INVOLVED A
HELMET CONNECTED DIRECTLY TO THE MOUTH,
PULLING IT OPEN PERMANENTLY. HOWEVER, THIS
PROVED IMPRACTICAL AS IT HINDERED THE
ACTOR'S ABILITY TO SPEAK. NEVERTHELESS,
JACKSON APPRECIATED THE VISUAL CONCEPT OF
THE ROBE FLOWING UP INTO THE HELMET, AND
THIS ELEMENT WAS RETAINED IN THE FINAL
DESIGN.

-

CONTRARY TO POPULAR BELIEF, FRODO AND SAM'S JOURNEY THROUGH MORDOR TO MOUNT DOOM IS CONDENSED INTO THREE CHAPTERS IN THE BOOK "THE RETURN OF THE KING." THEIR ADDITIONAL SCENES, SUCH AS THE ENCOUNTER WITH SHELOB AND FRODO'S CAPTURE BY THE ORCS, ACTUALLY OCCUR IN "THE TWO TOWERS." THE SECOND HALF OF "THE TWO TOWERS" EXCLUSIVELY FOCUSES ON FRODO AND SAM'S EXPLOITS. MEANWHILE, THE FIRST HALF OF "THE TWO TOWERS" DELVES INTO THE ADVENTURES OF THE REMAINING MEMBERS OF THE FELLOWSHIP. THE NARRATIVE THEN SHIFTS BACK TO THEIR STORY IN THE FIRST HALF OF "THE RETURN OF THE KING" AND ONLY RESUMES FRODO AND SAM'S TALE IN THE SECOND HALF. TO MAINTAIN ACCURATE TIMELINES AND PROVIDE ADEQUATE SCREEN TIME FOR FRODO AND SAM, SEVERAL CHAPTERS FROM THE END OF "THE TWO TOWERS" WERE INCORPORATED INTO THE SCRIPT FOR "THE RETURN OF THE KING."

-

MINAS TIRITH AND ITS SURROUNDINGS IN THE FILM ARE A COMBINATION OF VARIOUS LOCATIONS. THE SEVENTH TIER WAS A METICULOUSLY CRAFTED BACKLOT SET AT THREE FOOT SIX STUDIOS. THE INTRICATE STREETS WERE CONSTRUCTED IN A LABYRINTHINE SET WITHIN THE SAME ROCK QUARRY THAT SERVED AS THE HELM'S DEEP LOCATION. PELENNOR FIELDS, THE SITE OF THE EPIC BATTLE, SPANNED A VAST OPEN FIELD IN TWIZEL. OSGILIATH, ANOTHER SIGNIFICANT SETTING, WAS BROUGHT TO LIFE THROUGH A CAREFULLY DESIGNED BACKLOT SET. THE GRANDEUR OF OSGILIATH AND MINAS TIRITH WAS CAPTURED IN METICULOUSLY CRAFTED MODELS, WHILE THE MAJESTIC MOUNTAIN RANGES WERE DIGITALLY CREATED USING COMPOSITE PHOTOGRAPHS TAKEN FROM DIFFERENT REGIONS OF NEW ZEALAND.

-

THE ENDING SCENE OF THE FILM, WHERE SAM
RETURNS HOME AND IS JOYFULLY GREETED BY HIS
WIFE AND TWO CHILDREN, HOLDS A
HEARTWARMING TOUCH OF REALITY. THE OLDEST
CHILD PORTRAYED IN THE FILM IS ACTUALLY
SEAN ASTIN'S OWN CHILD, SEAMLESSLY
BLENDING THE REALM OF MIDDLE-EARTH WITH
THE PERSONAL LIVES OF THE ACTORS.

-

THE LORD OF THE RINGS TRILOGY ACHIEVED A
REMARKABLE FEAT BY WINNING THE SCIENCE
FICTION ACHIEVEMENT AWARD (HUGO AWARD)
FOR BEST DRAMATIC PRESENTATION, LONG FORM
IN 2004. THIS ACCOMPLISHMENT MARKED THE
FIRST INSTANCE OF A WORK SECURING TOP
MOVIE HONORS IN BOTH THE PRESTIGIOUS
OSCARS AND THE RENOWNED HUGOS.
FURTHERMORE, GOLLUM'S "PROFANE
ACCEPTANCE SPEECH" DELIVERED AT THE MTV
MOVIE AWARDS EARNED THE HUGO AWARD FOR
BEST DRAMATIC PRESENTATION, SHORT FORM.

-

IN A 2005 AUSTRALIAN MOVIE POLL, WHEN THE TRILOGY IS CONSIDERED AS A WHOLE, IT WAS VOTED AS THE BEST MOVIE OF ALL TIME BY AUDIENCES. THIS TREMENDOUS RECOGNITION UNDERSCORES THE TIMELESS IMPACT AND ENDURING LEGACY OF THE LORD OF THE RINGS ON THE CINEMATIC LANDSCAPE.

-

SAMWISE GAMGEE, THE LOYAL COMPANION TO FRODO, POSSESSES A UNIQUE SKILL DESPITE BEING LEFT-HANDED. HE DEMONSTRATES PROFICIENCY IN SWORD FIGHTING WITH BOTH HIS LEFT AND RIGHT HANDS, SHOWCASING HIS ADAPTABILITY AND VERSATILITY IN COMBAT.

-

THE EXTENDED EDITION DVD OF THE FILM OFFERS AN EXCLUSIVE TREAT FOR FANS. IT FEATURES A POIGNANT SONG TITLED "THE HOUSE OF HEALING" OR "ARWEN'S SONG," COMPOSED BY HOWARD SHORE AND PERFORMED BY LIV TYLER. THIS BEAUTIFUL COMPOSITION, HOWEVER, DID NOT MAKE IT INTO THE THEATRICAL VERSION, MAKING IT A CHERISHED ADDITION TO THE EXTENDED CUT.

FOR BERNARD HILL, THIS FILM MARKS HIS THIRD APPEARANCE IN A MOVIE THAT ACHIEVED THE DISTINCTION OF WINNING BOTH THE BEST PICTURE AND BEST DIRECTOR OSCARS. HE PREVIOUSLY EXPERIENCED THIS ACCOLADE WITH HIS ROLES IN THE ACCLAIMED FILMS "GANDHI" (1982) AND "TITANIC" (1997). THIS NOTABLE ACHIEVEMENT ATTESTS TO HILL'S REMARKABLE TALENT AND HIS KNACK FOR BEING PART OF EXCEPTIONAL CINEMATIC ENDEAVORS ACROSS DIFFERENT DECADES.

-

SAURON, THE TRUE LORD OF THE RINGS, IS NEVER EXPLICITLY MENTIONED AS SUCH IN THE FILMS. HOWEVER, THERE IS A BRIEF IMPLICATION IN "THE LORD OF THE RINGS: THE FELLOWSHIP OF THE RING" (2001) WHEN GANDALF INFORMS SARUMAN THAT THERE IS ONLY ONE WHO CAN WIELD THE RING AND THAT HE DOES NOT SHARE POWER. IN THE VAST LORE OF MIDDLE-EARTH, SAURON, DISGUISED AS ANNATAR, GUIDED THE ELVES IN CREATING THE RINGS OF POWER. HE THEN FORGED THE ONE RING, EXERTING CONTROL OVER ALL OTHER RINGS AND ESTABLISHING HIMSELF AS THE ULTIMATE LORD OF THE RINGS.

AMONG THE THREE MOVIES THAT HAVE WON ELEVEN ACADEMY AWARDS, "THE LORD OF THE RINGS" STANDS ALONE IN NOT RECEIVING ANY ACTING NOMINATIONS. WHILE THE TRILOGY GARNERED NUMEROUS ACCOLADES FOR ITS CINEMATIC ACHIEVEMENTS, ITS RECOGNITION PRIMARILY FOCUSED ON OTHER ASPECTS, SUCH AS DIRECTING, VISUAL EFFECTS, AND MUSIC.

-

SAMWISE GAMGEE, FROM THE FELLOWSHIP OF THE RING, HOLDS A UNIQUE DISTINCTION IN THE FILM SERIES. HE IS THE FIRST CHARACTER INTRODUCED IN THE EXTENDED VERSION OF THE FIRST FILM AND ALSO APPEARS IN THE CONCLUDING SCENES OF THE LAST FILM. SAM'S ENDURING PRESENCE THROUGHOUT THE TRILOGY SYMBOLIZES HIS UNWAVERING LOYALTY AND UNWAVERING DEDICATION TO FRODO'S QUEST.

-

FOLLOWING THE PRECEDENT SET BY "THE GODFATHER PART II" (1974), "THE LORD OF THE RINGS" BECAME THE FIRST SEQUEL SINCE THEN TO CAPTURE THE COVETED BEST PICTURE OSCAR. THIS REMARKABLE ACHIEVEMENT SOLIDIFIES THE TRILOGY'S PLACE IN CINEMATIC HISTORY AND RECOGNIZES ITS UNPARALLELED IMPACT ON THE FILM INDUSTRY.

-

SIMILAR TO THE PRODUCTION OF "THE LORD OF THE RINGS: THE TWO TOWERS" (2002), ADDITIONAL SCENES WERE FILMED IN NEW ZEALAND IN 2003 TO ENHANCE THE NARRATIVE. THIS APPROACH ALLOWED THE FILMMAKERS TO FINE-TUNE THE STORY AND ADD NEW SEQUENCES TO ENRICH THE VIEWER'S EXPERIENCE.

-

ALISON DOODY, KNOWN FOR HER ROLE IN THE INDIANA JONES FRANCHISE, WAS APPROACHED BY SIR PETER JACKSON TO PORTRAY EOWYN IN "THE LORD OF THE RINGS" TRILOGY. HOWEVER, SHE HAD TO DECLINE THE OFFER DUE TO HER PREGNANCY AND THE EXTENSIVE SIXTEEN-MONTH COMMITMENT REQUIRED FOR THE ROLE.

-

TO BRING LIFE TO THE GALLOPING HORSEBACK ARMY, WHICH PREDOMINANTLY RELIED ON CGI, THE FILMMAKERS UTILIZED MOTION-CAPTURE TECHNOLOGY. BY CAPTURING FOOTAGE OF A HORSE IN A MOTION-CAPTURE SUIT, THEY ACHIEVED A REALISTIC DEPICTION OF THE HORSES' MOVEMENTS AND BEHAVIORS.

-

ON JUNE 19TH, 2020, THE ESTEEMED ACTOR IAN HOLM, WHO PORTRAYED BILBO IN BOTH TRILOGIES, PASSED AWAY AT THE AGE OF 88. PRIOR TO HIS DEMISE, A ZOOM REUNION ORGANIZED BY JOSH GAD BROUGHT TOGETHER A SIGNIFICANT PORTION OF THE CAST. ALTHOUGH IAN HOLM COULDN'T ATTEND DUE TO HIS ILLNESS, HE CONVEYED HIS WARM WISHES TO THE GATHERING THROUGH A HEARTFELT LETTER SIGNED "HOBBIT HOLM."

-

A CONVERSATION BETWEEN GIMLI AND LEGOLAS HINTS AT THE TURMOIL FACED BY THE DWARVEN KINGDOM OF EREBOR AND ITS ALLIES DURING THE SIEGE OF MINAS TIRITH. GIMLI EXPRESSES HIS DESIRE TO SUMMON A LEGION OF DWARVES TO SUPPORT THE ROHIRRIM'S MARCH ON GONDOR. HOWEVER, LEGOLAS WARNS THAT WAR MAY ALREADY BE RAVAGING THEIR LANDS, POSSIBLY REFERRING TO THE EASTERLINGS' ASSAULT ON EREBOR, AN EVENT OCCURRING OFF-SCREEN CONCURRENTLY WITH THE SIEGE OF MINAS TIRITH.

-

THE DAY OF THE FILM'S PREMIERE IN NEW ZEALAND WAS A MOMENTOUS OCCASION THAT CAPTIVATED THE NATION. BOTH MAJOR TELEVISION NETWORKS TEMPORARILY SUSPENDED THEIR REGULAR PROGRAMMING TO PROVIDE LIVE COVERAGE OF THE PREMIERE, HIGHLIGHTING THE SIGNIFICANT CULTURAL IMPACT OF THE EPIC EVENT.

-

EOWYN, IN THE EXTENDED EDITION, SHARES WITH ARAGORN A DREAM SHE HAD ABOUT A COLOSSAL WAVE. INTERESTINGLY, J.R.R. TOLKIEN, IN A 1964 INTERVIEW, MENTIONED A RECURRING NIGHTMARE HE EXPERIENCED—A VISION OF AN OVERWHELMING WAVE ENGULFING THE LAND. HE REFERRED TO THIS AS HIS "ATLANTIS COMPLEX."

-

THE ORIGINAL CUT OF THE FILM HAD A RUNTIME OF 4 AND A 1/4 HOURS, BUT IT TOOK A YEAR TO TRIM IT DOWN TO A FINAL DURATION OF 3 HOURS AND 12 MINUTES. THE METICULOUS EDITING PROCESS AIMED TO STREAMLINE THE NARRATIVE WHILE PRESERVING THE ESSENCE OF THE EPIC STORY.

DURING THE INTENSE BATTLE OF PELENNOR FIELDS, A HAUNTING CHOIR CAN BE HEARD. THE LYRICS OF THIS CHORAL COMPOSITION DIRECTLY CORRESPOND TO EOWYN'S IMPENDING DUEL WITH THE WITCH KING, WITH SOME LINES DIRECTLY QUOTED FROM THE BOOK. TRANSLATED TO ENGLISH, THE LYRICS VIVIDLY DEPICT THE FATEFUL CONFRONTATION AND ITS AFTERMATH, SYMBOLIZING THE BRAVERY AND RESILIENCE OF EOWYN.

-

THE FIRST 30 MINUTES OF THE FILM, INCLUDING THE INITIAL STAGES OF SAM AND FRODO'S JOURNEY, DRAW HEAVILY FROM "THE TWO TOWERS" NOVEL. THIS CREATIVE DECISION ENSURED A SEAMLESS CONTINUATION OF THE STORY AND ALLOWED FOR A COMPREHENSIVE PORTRAYAL OF THE CHARACTERS' EXPERIENCES.

-

IN THE INITIAL CAST LIST FOR THE MOVIE, WI KUKI KAA WAS LISTED TO APPEAR AS A CHARACTER NAMED GHÂN-BURI-GHÂN. IN THE BOOK, GHÂN-BURI-GHÂN IS THE CHIEFTAIN OF THE WOSES, A GROUP OF UNTAMED MEN RESIDING IN THE DRUADAN FOREST OF GONDOR. THEY OFFER THEIR AID TO THE ROHIRRIM DURING THEIR PASSAGE. HOWEVER, GHÂN-BURI-GHÂN DOES NOT MAKE AN APPEARANCE IN EITHER THE THEATRICAL OR EXTENDED EDITIONS OF THE FILM, NOR IS THERE ANY MENTION OF HIS CHARACTER.

-

THE AWE-INSPIRING LIGHTNING STORM EFFECTS SEEN IN THE MOVIE WERE DERIVED FROM ACTUAL NEWS FOOTAGE CAPTURED IN LAWRENCE, KANSAS. BY INCORPORATING REAL-LIFE ELEMENTS, THE FILMMAKERS ACHIEVED A HEIGHTENED SENSE OF REALISM AND INTENSITY IN PORTRAYING THE STORMY ATMOSPHERE OF MIDDLE-EARTH.

-

THE ICONIC "WILHELM SCREAM" SOUND EFFECT, KNOWN FOR ITS RECURRING USE IN FILMS, CAN BE HEARD IN MULTIPLE INSTANCES THROUGHOUT "THE LORD OF THE RINGS" TRILOGY. IN THIS MOVIE, THE SCREAM CAN BE HEARD WHEN LEGOLAS KNOCKS A SOUTHRON OFF AN OLIPHAUNT, WHEN AN OLIPHAUNT WRANGLER IS STRUCK BY ÉOMER'S SPEAR BEFORE THE COLLISION OF TWO MÛMAKIL DURING THE BATTLE OF PELENNOR FIELDS, AND WHEN A FELL BEAST SNATCHES A SOLDIER FROM HIS HORSE DURING THE RETREAT FROM OSGILIATH. THIS SOUND EFFECT HAS BECOME A BELOVED EASTER EGG FOR MANY MOVIE ENTHUSIASTS.

-

THE CHARACTER ORIGINALLY WRITTEN AS IROLAS WAS INTENDED TO BE BEREGOND, A CHARACTER FROM THE BOOK. WHILE IROLAS DOES NOT APPEAR IN THE BOOK, HE IS IDENTIFIED AS BEREGOND'S BROTHER (SPELLED "IORLAS" IN THE BOOK). INTERESTINGLY, "IORLAS" TRANSLATES TO "OLD LEAF" IN SINDARIN ELVISH, WHEREAS "IROLAS" DOES NOT HOLD A SPECIFIC MEANING.

-

THE ENCHANTING THEME THAT ACCOMPANIES GANDALF'S RESCUE OF FRODO AND SAM FROM MOUNT DOOM FEATURES SINDARIN (ELVISH) LYRICS. THE TRANSLATED LYRICS EVOKE A SENSE OF ETHEREAL BEAUTY AND REFLECTION, EXPRESSING SENTIMENTS SUCH AS BEING LIFTED UP IN A DREAM, EMERGING FROM DARKNESS, AND PONDERING THE STATE OF THE WORLD.

-

THIS FILM JOINS THE RANKS OF PRESTIGIOUS MOVIES LASTING OVER 3 HOURS TO HAVE WON THE COVETED OSCAR FOR BEST PICTURE. IT FOLLOWS THE FOOTSTEPS OF ICONIC FILMS LIKE "GONE WITH THE WIND" (1939), "AROUND THE WORLD IN 80 DAYS" (1956), "BEN-HUR" (1959), "LAWRENCE OF ARABIA" (1962), "THE GODFATHER PART II" (1974), "THE DEER HUNTER" (1978), "GANDHI" (1982), "DANCES WITH WOLVES" (1990), "SCHINDLER'S LIST" (1993), AND "TITANIC" (1997).

-

IN THE EXTENDED EDITION, A SIGNIFICANT
PALANTIR SCENE UNFOLDS BETWEEN ARAGORN
AND SAURON. DURING THIS SEQUENCE, THERE IS
A BRIEF GLIMPSE OF SAURON HOLDING THE
PALANTIR IN HIS ARMORED FORM, SUGGESTING
HIS RETURN TO A HUMANOID SHAPE, HINTING AT
THE EXTENT OF HIS POWER AND PRESENCE.

-

WITH A RUNTIME OF 201 MINUTES, THIS FILM
HOLDS THE DISTINCTION OF BEING THE
LONGEST MOVIE TO SURPASS THE REMARKABLE
MILESTONE OF GROSSING OVER $1 BILLION
WORLDWIDE (WITHOUT ADJUSTING FOR
INFLATION). ITS EPIC LENGTH CAPTIVATED
AUDIENCES WORLDWIDE, CONTRIBUTING TO ITS
IMMENSE SUCCESS.

-

TO ENHANCE THE VISUAL IMPACT AND CREATE MORE FORMIDABLE ANTAGONISTS, DIRECTOR PETER JACKSON FELT THAT THE MORDOR ORCS SEEMED LACKING COMPARED TO THE POWERFUL URUK-HAI INTRODUCED IN THE SECOND FILM. CONSEQUENTLY, WETA WORKSHOP DEVELOPED GROTESQUE AND INTIMIDATING "ÜBER ORCS" KNOWN AS GOTHMOG. ADDITIONALLY, THE WITCH-KING UNDERWENT A REDESIGN, AND HIS SCENES WERE RESHOT TO ELIMINATE CONFUSION AMONG NON-READERS REGARDING SAURON'S PRESENCE ON THE BATTLEFIELD.

-

AN INTRIGUING DETAIL CAN BE OBSERVED IN THE DISTINCTION BETWEEN SMEAGOL AND GOLLUM. SPECIFICALLY, SMEAGOL'S PUPILS APPEAR MORE DILATED THAN GOLLUM'S. THIS SUBTLE CHANGE IN PUPIL SIZE ACCENTUATES THE TRANSFORMATION BETWEEN PERSONALITIES DURING THE REFLECTION DIALOGUE SCENE, UNDERSCORING THE DUALITY OF THE CHARACTER.

-

JED BROPHY, WHO PORTRAYED A "FEATURED ORC," MADE APPEARANCES IN PREVIOUS FILMS WITHIN THE MIDDLE-EARTH FRANCHISE. HE PLAYED AN ORC IN "THE TWO TOWERS" (2002) AND ALSO APPEARED IN "KING KONG" (2005) AND THE SIR PETER JACKSON-PRODUCED "DISTRICT 9" (2009). BROPHY LATER RECEIVED A PROMINENT ROLE AS NORI IN "THE HOBBIT: AN UNEXPECTED JOURNEY" (2012), "THE HOBBIT: THE DESOLATION OF SMAUG" (2013), AND "THE HOBBIT: THE BATTLE OF THE FIVE ARMIES" (2014).

-

AS EACH CHARACTER ENTERS THE ROOM TO SEE FRODO, MERRY, AND PIPPIN, THE MUSIC UNDERGOES SUBTLE CHANGES TO REFLECT THEIR PRESENCE. THE ENTRANCE OF MERRY AND PIPPIN BRINGS A LIGHTER TONE, WITH THE FAMILIAR TIN WHISTLE BECOMING MORE PROMINENT. WHEN GIMLI ENTERS, THE MUSIC GROWS LOUDER AND STRONGER, MAINTAINING ITS JOYFUL AND LIVELY QUALITY. LEGOLAS' ENTRANCE BRINGS A MORE SERIOUS AND ELEGANT THEME, HIGHLIGHTING HIS REGAL DEMEANOR. ARAGORN'S ARRIVAL CARRIES A MAJESTIC AND ROYAL AURA. AS THE SHOT PANS OUT TO REVEAL THE ENTIRE FELLOWSHIP, THE MUSIC SWELLS INTO AN EPIC ORCHESTRAL MOMENT. FINALLY, SAM'S ENTRANCE LEADS TO A QUIETING OF THE MUSIC, TRANSITIONING INTO A SOFTER AND SLOWER VERSION OF THE BELOVED "CONCERNING HOBBITS" THEME.

-

THE ESTEEMED CAST OF THE FILM BOASTS EIGHT OSCAR WINNERS: CATE BLANCHETT, SIR PETER JACKSON, ANDREW LESNIE, BRET MCKENZIE, CHRISTIAN RIVERS, MICHAEL SEMANICK, HOWARD SHORE, AND SIR RICHARD TAYLOR. ADDITIONALLY, THE CAST INCLUDES FIVE OSCAR NOMINEES: SEAN ASTIN, SIR IAN HOLM, SIR IAN MCKELLEN, VIGGO MORTENSEN, AND, IN THE EXTENDED EDITION DVD, BRAD DOURIF.

-

ANDY SERKIS'S TRANSFORMATION INTO GOLLUM INVOLVED A COMPLEX PROSTHETIC MAKE-UP PROCESS KNOWN AS THE "FALL OF SMEAGOL." APPLYING THIS FINAL STAGE OF MAKE-UP BEFORE THE CGI EFFECTS REQUIRED AN ARDUOUS FIVE-HOUR PROCESS. INTERESTINGLY, THIS IS THE SAME DURATION IT TOOK TO APPLY ARNOLD SCHWARZENEGGER'S DAMAGED TERMINATOR MAKE-UP IN "TERMINATOR 2: JUDGMENT DAY" (1991).

-

AMONG J.R.R. TOLKIEN FANS, THE WITCH-KING, THE LEADER OF THE NAZGÛL, IS COMMONLY REFERRED TO AS ANGMAR, AFTER THE REALM HE

FOUNDED AND RULED. ALTHOUGH HIS TRUE NAME REMAINS UNKNOWN IN THE LORE, FANS OFTEN IDENTIFY HIM AS EITHER ONE OF THE THREE BLACK NÚMENÓREANS WHO BECAME NAZGÛL OR AS ISILMO, A NÚMENÓREAN PRINCE AND FATHER OF TAR-MINASTIR. IN NON-CANONICAL SOURCES SUCH AS THE MIDDLE-EARTH ROLE-PLAYING GAME, HE HAS BEEN NAMED "ER-MURAZOR," WHILE THE ANGBAND COMPUTER GAME REFERS TO HIM AS "MURAZOR, THE WITCH-KING OF ANGMAR."

-

THE WAY LEGOLAS CAUSES A MÛMAKIL (OLIPHAUNT) TO FALL BY PIERCING ITS SKULL WITH ARROWS IS REMINISCENT OF THE ICONIC SCENE IN "THE EMPIRE STRIKES BACK" (1980) WHERE REBEL PILOTS TAKE DOWN AT-AT WALKERS USING HARPOONS AND TOW CABLES.

-

THE FIRST CHARGE OF THE ROHIRRIM AT THE BATTLE OF PELENNOR FIELDS LEAVES BLACK ORC BLOOD ON THEODEN'S SWORD. THIS DETAIL ALIGNS WITH J.R.R. TOLKIEN'S BOOKS AND REFLECTS SIMILAR INSTANCES OF BLOODSTAINED SWORDS IN THE PREVIOUS FILMS.

-

"THE RETURN OF THE KING" IS NOT ONLY THE TITLE OF THE THIRD FILM IN "THE LORD OF THE RINGS" TRILOGY BUT ALSO A GRAPHIC NOVEL IN THE X-MEN SERIES. IN THE X-MEN CONTEXT, THE TITLE REFERS TO MAGNETO, A CHARACTER PORTRAYED BY SIR IAN MCKELLEN, WHO ALSO PLAYS GANDALF IN THE TRILOGY. THE X-MEN SERIES ALSO FEATURES A VILLAIN NAMED SAURON, ADDING AN INTRIGUING CONNECTION.

-

THIS FILM SHOWCASES AN IMPRESSIVE DISPLAY OF 1,489 VISUAL EFFECT SHOTS, WHICH IS NEARLY THREE TIMES THE NUMBER FOUND IN THE FIRST FILM AND ALMOST TWICE AS MANY AS THE SECOND. THE SIGNIFICANT INCREASE IN VISUAL EFFECTS HIGHLIGHTS THE GRANDEUR AND SCALE OF THE FINAL INSTALLMENT.

-

DURING GANDALF'S SLUMBER, PIPPIN TEMPORARILY REPLACES THE PALANTIR WITH A PITCHER. INTERESTINGLY, THIS PITCHER MAKES A LATER APPEARANCE IN MINAS TIRITH WHEN PIPPIN AND GANDALF ENGAGE IN A CONVERSATION AFTER VISITING THE STEWARD. THIS SUBTLE CONTINUITY DETAIL ADDS DEPTH TO THE FILM'S WORLD-BUILDING.

-

"THE RETURN OF THE KING" HOLDS THE DISTINCTION OF RECEIVING 11 OSCAR NOMINATIONS, THE MOST NOMINATIONS FOR A FILM WITHOUT AN ACTING NOMINATION. THIS RECORD-BREAKING ACHIEVEMENT HAS SINCE BEEN MATCHED BY TWO OTHER FILMS, NAMELY "HUGO" (2011) AND "LIFE OF PI" (2012).

AS THE FIRST FANTASY FILM TO WIN THE
ACADEMY AWARD FOR BEST PICTURE, "THE
RETURN OF THE KING" MADE HISTORY IN THE
WORLD OF CINEMA. NOTABLY, IT REMAINED THE
ONLY MOVIE FOR 14 YEARS TO ACHIEVE THIS
FEAT WITHOUT BEING INCLUDED IN THE
NATIONAL BOARD OF REVIEW'S TOP TEN FILMS
OF THE YEAR, UNTIL "THE SHAPE OF WATER"
(2017) REPLICATED THE ACCOMPLISHMENT IN
2017.

-

THE UNDEAD ARMY THAT ARAGORN RECRUITS
CONSISTS OF GLOWING GREEN GHOSTS WHOSE
SPIRIT FORMS HAVE DECAYED DUE TO THEIR AGE.
PETER JACKSON'S PREVIOUS FILM, "THE
FRIGHTENERS," ALSO FEATURED SIMILAR
GHOSTLY CHARACTERS, SHOWCASING THE
DIRECTOR'S THEMATIC INTEREST IN
SUPERNATURAL ENTITIES.

-

REMARKABLY, "THE RETURN OF THE KING" BECAME THE 20TH FILM TO BOTH WIN THE BEST PICTURE OSCAR AND BECOME THE HIGHEST-GROSSING FILM OF THE YEAR. THIS DISTINCTION PLACES IT IN ESTEEMED COMPANY ALONGSIDE OTHER ACCLAIMED MOVIES LIKE "BROADWAY MELODY" (1929), "MUTINY ON THE BOUNTY" (1935), "THE GREAT ZIEGFELD" (1936), "GONE WITH THE WIND" (1939), AND "RAIN MAN" (1988), TO NAME A FEW.

-

"THE LORD OF THE RINGS: THE RETURN OF THE KING" HOLDS THE DISTINCTION OF HAVING THE LONGEST TITLE AMONG ALL THE FILMS THAT HAVE WON THE BEST PICTURE OSCAR. WITH A TOTAL OF THIRTY-FIVE LETTERS, IT SURPASSES THE PREVIOUS RECORD HELD BY "AROUND THE WORLD IN 80 DAYS" (1956), WHICH HAD TWENTY-SIX LETTERS. ADDITIONALLY, IT ALSO SET THE RECORD FOR THE MOST WORDS IN A BEST PICTURE TITLE, TOTALING TEN WORDS.

-

CRAIG PARKER PROVIDED THE VOICE FOR
GOTHMOG, A CHARACTER IN THE FILM,
ALTHOUGH HE IS NOT CREDITED FOR HIS ROLE.
PARKER PREVIOUSLY PORTRAYED HALDIR THE
ELF IN THE TWO PRECEDING FILMS OF THE
TRILOGY.

-

THIS FILM HAS SECURED A SPOT IN THE OFFICIAL
TOP 250 NARRATIVE FEATURE FILMS ON
LETTERBOXD, AN ONLINE COMMUNITY FOR FILM
ENTHUSIASTS. THE INCLUSION OF THE FILM IN
THIS PRESTIGIOUS LIST HIGHLIGHTS ITS
ENDURING POPULARITY AND RECOGNITION
AMONG AUDIENCES.

-

WHILE COMMONLY REFERRED TO AS "NOVELS,"
J.R.R. TOLKIEN PREFERRED TO DESCRIBE HIS
WORKS AS "HEROIC ROMANCES." TOLKIEN'S
PREFERENCE INDICATES THAT HE VIEWED HIS
STORIES AS BELONGING TO THE GENRE OF
HEROIC ROMANCE, WHICH FALLS WITHIN THE
BROADER CATEGORY OF NOVELS. THESE TERMS
ARE NOT MUTUALLY EXCLUSIVE BUT OFFER
DIFFERENT PERSPECTIVES ON HIS LITERARY
CREATIONS.

-

IN A NOTABLE SCENE, LEGOLAS CLIMBS ONTO
THE OLIPHAUNT, A MASSIVE CREATURE, WHERE
HE FACES RESISTANCE FROM THE ANIMAL'S
TRUNK AND TAIL, AS IT ATTEMPTS TO DISLODGE
HIM. THIS SEQUENCE SHOWCASES LEGOLAS'S
AGILITY AND THE CHALLENGES HE ENCOUNTERS
WHILE ENGAGING WITH FORMIDABLE FOES.

-

"THE LORD OF THE RINGS: THE RETURN OF THE KING" BECAME THE NINTH FILM TO WIN THE ACADEMY AWARD FOR BEST PICTURE WITHOUT RECEIVING A SINGLE ACTING NOMINATION. SINCE THEN, TEN MORE MOVIES HAVE ACHIEVED THIS DISTINCTION, INCLUDING "WINGS" (1927), "ALL QUIET ON THE WESTERN FRONT" (1930), "GRAND HOTEL" (1932), "THE GREATEST SHOW ON EARTH" (1952), "AROUND THE WORLD IN 80 DAYS" (1956), "GIGI" (1958), "THE LAST EMPEROR" (1987), "BRAVEHEART" (1995), AND "SLUMDOG MILLIONAIRE" (2008).

-

THE MYTHOLOGY CREATED BY J.R.R. TOLKIEN HAS INSPIRED NUMEROUS BLACK METAL BANDS, LEADING TO THEIR ADOPTION OF NAMES REFERENCING PLACES AND CHARACTERS FROM HIS WORKS. NOTABLE EXAMPLES INCLUDE NORWEGIAN BANDS LIKE GORGOROTH, BURZUM, AND MORGUL, SWEDISH BAND AMON AMARTH (NAMED AFTER MOUNT DOOM), AND DUTCH BAND CARACH ANGREN (NAMED AFTER ISENMOUTHE).

-

THE SDDS (SONY DYNAMIC DIGITAL SOUND) 8 CHANNEL DECODERS USED IN CINEMAS DISPLAY THE TITLE OF THE MOVIE THEY ARE DECODING. INTERESTINGLY, CERTAIN REELS OF "THE LORD OF THE RINGS: THE RETURN OF THE KING" WERE LABELED AS "TILL DEATH FOR GLORY," WHILE OTHERS WERE LABELED AS "BEIJING CHICKEN." THESE ALTERNATE LABELS ADD AN AMUSING AND INTRIGUING ASPECT TO THE FILM'S PRODUCTION PROCESS.

-

J.R.R. TOLKIEN CLARIFIED THAT WHILE FELL BEASTS, SOMETIMES RESEMBLING PTEROSAURS, SHARE CERTAIN SIMILARITIES, THEY WERE NOT SPECIFICALLY INTENDED TO BE "PTERODACTYLIC" CREATURES. TOLKIEN ACKNOWLEDGED THE RESEMBLANCE BUT EMPHASIZED THAT FELL BEASTS DIFFER SIGNIFICANTLY FROM THE MODERN SCIENTIFIC UNDERSTANDING OF PTEROSAURS. IN HIS WORKS, FELL BEASTS ARE DEPICTED AS ENDOTHERMIC, HAIRY QUADRUPEDS RATHER THAN "FEATHERLESS BIRDS."

-

AMONG THE BEST PICTURE OSCAR NOMINEES THAT YEAR, THIS FILM STOOD OUT AS THE SOLE NOMINEE TO RECEIVE NOMINATIONS FOR BOTH BEST ORIGINAL SCORE AND BEST SONG. ITS RECOGNITION IN THESE CATEGORIES HIGHLIGHTS THE EXCEPTIONAL MUSICAL CONTRIBUTIONS THAT ENHANCED THE FILM'S OVERALL EXPERIENCE.

-

PRIOR TO 2022, THIS FILM WAS THE MOST RECENT BEST PICTURE WINNER AT THE ACADEMY AWARDS TO ACHIEVE A CLEAN SWEEP, SECURING VICTORIES IN ALL THE CATEGORIES IT WAS NOMINATED FOR. WHILE GRAND HOTEL (1932) WON ITS ONLY NOMINATION, THIS FILM IS ONE OF THE FIVE OUT OF SIX FILMS TO ACCOMPLISH THIS FEAT. THE OTHER FILMS THAT HAVE ACHIEVED A CLEAN SWEEP ARE WINGS (1927), IT HAPPENED ONE NIGHT (1934), GIGI (1958), THE LAST EMPEROR (1987), AND CODA (2021).

-

SIR CHRISTOPHER LEE AND BRAD DOURIF, BOTH TALENTED ACTORS, HAVE THE DISTINCTION OF APPEARING IN TWO BEST PICTURE-WINNING FILMS. SIR CHRISTOPHER LEE HAD A ROLE IN HAMLET (1948), WHILE BRAD DOURIF APPEARED IN ALGUIEN VOLÓ SOBRE EL NIDO DEL CUCO (1975). THEIR INVOLVEMENT IN MULTIPLE ACCLAIMED FILMS REFLECTS THEIR VERSATILITY AND CONTRIBUTION TO THE CINEMATIC WORLD.

-

ANDY SERKIS, RENOWNED FOR HIS MOTION-CAPTURE PERFORMANCES, PORTRAYED SUPREME LEADER SNOKE IN STAR WARS: EL DESPERTAR DE LA FUERZA (2015) AND STAR WARS: LOS ÚLTIMOS JEDI (2017). IT IS NOTEWORTHY THAT GEORGE LUCAS, THE CREATOR OF STAR WARS, ACKNOWLEDGED THE LORD OF THE RINGS AS A SIGNIFICANT INFLUENCE ON HIS ICONIC SPACE SAGA, SHOWCASING THE FAR-REACHING IMPACT OF TOLKIEN'S WORK.

-

ARAGORN, A CENTRAL CHARACTER IN THE FILM, ASSUMES THE ROLE OF THE LONG-AWAITED RETURNING KING IN A CITY THAT HAS BEEN GOVERNED BY STEWARDS. THE ARCHITECTURAL DESIGN OF THE CITY BEARS RESEMBLANCE TO ROME, PARTICULARLY WITH ITS TOP TIER BEARING A STRIKING RESEMBLANCE TO THE VATICAN. IT IS WORTH MENTIONING THAT J.R.R. TOLKIEN, A DEVOUT ROMAN CATHOLIC, MAY HAVE DRAWN INSPIRATION FROM HIS FAITH IN CREATING THIS SYMBOLIC REPRESENTATION.

-

JOHN NOBLE, AN ACTOR IN THE FILM, LATER PORTRAYED ANOTHER FICTIONAL FATHER FIGURE IN THE TV SERIES THE BOYS (2019). IN THIS SERIES, HE PLAYED THE ROLE OF SAMUEL BUTCHER, THE FATHER OF BILLY BUTCHER, PORTRAYED BY KARL URBAN. NOBLE'S ABILITY TO BRING DIVERSE FATHERLY CHARACTERS TO LIFE HIGHLIGHTS HIS VERSATILITY AS AN ACTOR.

-

TWO ACTORS FROM THIS FILM, BERNARD HILL AND JOHN RHYS-DAVIES, HAVE ALSO APPEARED IN MOVIES RELATED TO THE TITANIC. BERNARD HILL PORTRAYED CAPTAIN SMITH IN JAMES CAMERON'S "TITANIC," WHILE JOHN RHYS-DAVIES PLAYED THE CAPTAIN OF THE TITANIC'S SISTER SHIP BRITANNIC IN THE 2000 TELEVISION MOVIE "BRITANNIC." THIS CONNECTION ADDS AN INTERESTING OVERLAP BETWEEN THEIR ROLES IN DIFFERENT TITANIC-RELATED PROJECTS.

-

THE PRINTS OF THE FILM WERE DISTRIBUTED TO THEATERS USING THE CODE NAME "TIL DEATH FOR GLORY." THIS PRACTICE IS COMMON IN THE FILM INDUSTRY TO MAINTAIN SECRECY AND AVOID UNAUTHORIZED LEAKS OR EARLY REVEALS. THE USE OF A CODE NAME ADDS AN ELEMENT OF INTRIGUE AND PROTECTION TO THE FILM'S DISTRIBUTION PROCESS.

-

DURING THE SCENE WHERE ARAGORN REVEALS HIMSELF TO SAURON THROUGH THE PALANTIR, SAURON UTTERS THE ELVISH PHRASE "SILIVREN PENNA MIRIEL." THIS PHRASE IS DERIVED FROM THE POEM "A ELBERETH GILTHONIEL" FEATURED IN THE BOOKS AND TRANSLATES TO "WHITE-SPARKLING, FALLING DOWN JEWEL." THE SIGNIFICANCE OF THIS PHRASE IS HEIGHTENED WHEN, MOMENTS LATER, THE EVENSTAR JEWEL FALLS FROM ARAGORN'S NECK AND SHATTERS ON THE FLOOR, SYMBOLIZING A POWERFUL VISUAL REPRESENTATION OF THE PHRASE.

-

LEGOLAS, ONE OF THE MAIN CHARACTERS, IS DEPICTED WEARING A CROWN DURING ARAGORN'S CORONATION. THIS DETAIL HIGHLIGHTS LEGOLAS' LINEAGE AS THE SON OF THE ELVEN KING THRANDUIL, THUS ESTABLISHING HIS STATUS AS A PRINCE WITHIN THE ELVEN REALM. THE INCLUSION OF THE CROWN ADDS DEPTH TO LEGOLAS' CHARACTER AND EMPHASIZES HIS NOBLE HERITAGE.

-

THE FIRST SCENE INVOLVING HUMAN CHARACTERS TAKES PLACE IN THEODEN'S HALLS, WHERE HE TOASTS THE "VICTORIOUS DEAD." INTERESTINGLY, IT IS THE ACTUAL FORCE OF THE DEAD, THE ARMY OF THE DEAD, THAT ULTIMATELY EMERGES TRIUMPHANT DURING THE SIEGE OF MINAS TIRITH. THIS JUXTAPOSITION BETWEEN THE TOAST AND THE VICTORIOUS INTERVENTION OF THE DEAD ADDS A POWERFUL AND UNEXPECTED TWIST TO THE NARRATIVE.

-

THIS FILM HAS EARNED ITS PLACE AMONG THE
"1001 MOVIES YOU MUST SEE BEFORE YOU DIE," A
COMPILATION EDITED BY STEVEN SCHNEIDER.
THIS RECOGNITION ACKNOWLEDGES THE FILM'S
CULTURAL AND ARTISTIC SIGNIFICANCE,
SOLIDIFYING ITS STATUS AS A MUST-WATCH
CINEMATIC MASTERPIECE THAT CAPTIVATES
AUDIENCES ACROSS GENERATIONS.

-

FOR ACTOR BERNARD HILL, THIS FILM MARKS HIS
SECOND BEST PICTURE WIN, FOLLOWING GANDHI
(1982). NOTABLY, GANDHI FEATURED SIR
MICHAEL HORDERN, WHO PORTRAYED GANDALF
IN THE BBC RADIO ADAPTATION. FURTHERMORE,
THE CHARACTER MOHAMMED ALI JINNAH,
DEPICTED IN GANDHI, WAS PLAYED BY SIR
CHRISTOPHER LEE IN JINNAH (1998). THESE
CONNECTIONS BETWEEN THE ACTORS AND THEIR
ROLES IN DIFFERENT FILMS PROVIDE AN
INTRIGUING LINK WITHIN THEIR CAREERS.

-

IN A POIGNANT MOMENT, SAM TAKES ON THE ROLE OF SIMON OF CYRENE WHEN HE TELLS FRODO, "I CAN'T CARRY IT FOR YOU, BUT I CAN CARRY YOU." THIS REFERENCE ALLUDES TO SIMON OF CYRENE, WHO HELPED CARRY THE CROSS FOR JESUS DURING THE CRUCIFIXION. SAM'S SELFLESS ACT OF SUPPORTING FRODO PARALLELS SIMON'S ASSISTANCE TO JESUS, HIGHLIGHTING THE PROFOUND FRIENDSHIP AND UNWAVERING LOYALTY BETWEEN THE TWO CHARACTERS.

\-

JOHN RHYS-DAVIES, WHO PORTRAYED THE ORC GORBAG, CAN BE SEEN WEARING A PIECE OF GONDORIAN ARMOR ON HIS SHOULDER. THIS DETAIL SUGGESTS THAT GORBAG EITHER FOUGHT AGAINST SOLDIERS FROM MINAS TIRITH OR ACQUIRED LOOT FROM BATTLES AS A CAPTAIN. THE PRESENCE OF THE ARMOR ADDS DEPTH TO THE CHARACTER AND HINTS AT HIS INVOLVEMENT IN CONFLICTS RELATED TO GONDOR.

\-

DESPITE BEING THE OLDEST OF THE FOUR ACTORS PLAYING THE MAIN HOBBITS, BILLY BOYD'S CHARACTER, PIPPIN, IS ACTUALLY THE YOUNGEST AMONG THEM. THIS AGE DIFFERENCE HIGHLIGHTS THE ACTORS' ABILITY TO PORTRAY CHARACTERS YOUNGER THAN THEMSELVES CONVINCINGLY, SHOWCASING THEIR ACTING SKILLS AND THE IMMERSIVE NATURE OF THE FILM'S STORYTELLING.

-

IN 2004, SEVERAL CAST MEMBERS INCLUDING SEAN ASTIN, ANDY SERKIS, JOHN RHYS-DAVIES, SARAH MCLEOD, AND THOMAS ROBBINS ATTENDED THE ARMAGEDDON EXPO IN WELLINGTON, NEW ZEALAND. THE EVENT PROVIDED AN OPPORTUNITY FOR FANS TO MEET AND INTERACT WITH THE ACTORS, CREATING A MEMORABLE EXPERIENCE FOR BOTH THE CAST AND ATTENDEES.

-

THE FILM MARKS THE DEBUT OF ALI ASTIN, WHO LIKELY HAD A ROLE OR APPEARANCE IN THE PRODUCTION. THIS DEBUT REPRESENTS AN EXCITING MILESTONE IN ALI ASTIN'S ACTING CAREER, PROVIDING A PLATFORM FOR HER TO SHOWCASE HER TALENTS AND ESTABLISH HERSELF WITHIN THE INDUSTRY.

-

DURING THE ACADEMY AWARDS CEREMONY, SIR PETER JACKSON, THE DIRECTOR OF THE FILM, RECEIVED THE BEST PICTURE AWARD FROM ESTEEMED FILMMAKER STEVEN SPIELBERG. NOTABLY, SPIELBERG HAD PREVIOUSLY WON BOTH BEST DIRECTOR AND BEST PICTURE FOR HIS FILM SCHINDLER'S LIST (1993) TEN YEARS EARLIER. FURTHERMORE, SCHINDLER'S LIST FEATURED BEN KINGSLEY, WHO HAD SHARED THE SCREEN WITH BERNARD HILL IN GANDHI (1982), A FILM THAT ALSO EARNED BEST DIRECTOR AND BEST PICTURE AWARDS FOR RICHARD ATTENBOROUGH. THESE CONNECTIONS HIGHLIGHT THE INTERPLAY OF TALENT AND RECOGNITION WITHIN THE FILM INDUSTRY.

-

IAN HOLM AND BERNARD HILL APPEARED CONSECUTIVELY IN TWO BEST PICTURE-WINNING FILMS DURING THE 1980S. IAN HOLM HAD A ROLE IN CHARIOTS OF FIRE (1981), WHILE BERNARD HILL APPEARED IN GANDHI (1982). NOTABLY, BOTH FILMS ALSO FEATURED ACTORS IAN CHARLESON AND JOHN GIELGUD, FURTHER ESTABLISHING CONNECTIONS AND SHARED EXPERIENCES AMONG THE CAST MEMBERS.

-

JOHN RHYS-DAVIES HAD A ROLE IN THE MINISERIES WAR AND REMEMBRANCE (1988), WHICH ALSO INCLUDED ACTORS ROBERT STEPHENS AND PETER VAUGHAN. STEPHENS AND VAUGHAN, IN TURN, WERE PART OF THE BBC RADIO ADAPTATION OF THE LORD OF THE RINGS, PORTRAYING THE CHARACTERS ARAGORN AND DENETHOR, RESPECTIVELY. THIS CONNECTION SHOWCASES THE ACTORS' INVOLVEMENT IN DIFFERENT PROJECTS RELATED TO TOLKIEN'S WORK.

-

SEAN ASTIN (SAMWISE GAMGEE) AND BILLY BOYD (PEREGRIN "PIPPIN" TOOK) APPEARED IN THE FILMS LAS BRUJAS DE OZ (2011) AND DOROTHY AND THE WITCHES OF OZ (2011). THESE APPEARANCES HIGHLIGHT THE ACTORS' PARTICIPATION IN OTHER FANTASY-THEMED PRODUCTIONS BEYOND THE LORD OF THE RINGS, OFFERING FANS THE OPPORTUNITY TO SEE THEM IN DIFFERENT ROLES WITHIN THE GENRE.

-

BERNARD HILL'S FIRST FILM TO WIN THE BEST PICTURE AWARD WAS GANDHI (1982), WHICH ALSO FEATURED NOTABLE ACTORS AMRISH PURI AND ROSHAN SETH. FOLLOWING THEIR APPEARANCE IN GANDHI, PURI AND SETH WENT ON TO COLLABORATE AGAIN IN INDIANA JONES Y EL TEMPLO MALDITO (1984). ADDITIONALLY, PHILIP STONE, WHO PROVIDED THE VOICE FOR THEODEN IN EL SEÑOR DE LOS ANILLOS (1978), ALSO APPEARED IN INDIANA JONES Y EL TEMPLO MALDITO, ESTABLISHING FURTHER CONNECTIONS AMONG THE CAST MEMBERS.

-

THE INDIVIDUAL NOVEL ON WHICH THIS MOVIE
WAS BASED, J.R.R. TOLKIEN'S "THE RETURN OF THE
KING," MADE AN APPEARANCE IN THE BEDROOM
OF CONRAD JARRETT (PLAYED BY TIMOTHY
HUTTON) IN THE FILM GENTE CORRIENTE (1980).
COINCIDENTALLY, BOTH GENTE CORRIENTE AND
THE MOVIE BASED ON TOLKIEN'S NOVEL WON
THE PRESTIGIOUS ACADEMY AWARD FOR BEST
PICTURE, SHOWCASING THE DIVERSE RANGE OF
STORIES THAT CAPTURE THE ATTENTION OF
AUDIENCES AND CRITICS ALIKE.

-

CHRISTOPHER TOLKIEN, SON OF J.R.R. TOLKIEN, PLAYED AN INSTRUMENTAL ROLE IN THE CREATION OF THE MAPS FEATURED IN THE BOOKS. AS HIS FATHER WAS UNABLE TO AFFORD A SECRETARY AT THE TIME, CHRISTOPHER TOOK ON THE RESPONSIBILITY OF DRAWING THE MAPS HIMSELF. DURING HIS SERVICE AS A FIGHTER PILOT STATIONED AT A SOUTH AFRICAN AIR BASE IN 1943, CHRISTOPHER RECEIVED REGULAR LETTERS FROM HIS FATHER, PROVIDING UPDATES ON THE PROGRESS OF THE BOOKS. HE OFTEN FOUND SOLACE IN READING A CHAPTER UPON LANDING, HIGHLIGHTING THE UNIQUE CIRCUMSTANCES SURROUNDING THE DEVELOPMENT OF TOLKIEN'S EPIC TALES.

-

BRAD DOURIF, KNOWN FOR HIS ROLE IN THIS FILM, HAD HIS FIRST EXPERIENCE WITH A BEST PICTURE WINNER IN ALGUIEN VOLÓ SOBRE EL NIDO DEL CUCO (1975). NOTABLY, THIS FILM ALSO FEATURED SCATMAN CROTHERS AND JACK NICHOLSON, WITH AN UNCREDITED CAMEO BY NICHOLSON'S THEN-GIRLFRIEND, ANJELICA HUSTON. ANJELICA'S FATHER, JOHN HUSTON, LENT HIS VOICE TO THE CHARACTER OF GANDALF IN EL RETORNO DEL REY (1980). CROTHERS AND NICHOLSON SHARED THE SCREEN AGAIN IN EL RESPLANDOR (1980), WHICH ALSO INCLUDED PHILIP STONE, THE VOICE BEHIND THEODEN IN EL SEÑOR DE LOS ANILLOS (1978).

-

SIR CHRISTOPHER LEE'S VOICE WAS DUBBED BY OMERO ANTONUTTI IN THE ITALIAN VERSION OF THE MOVIE. THIS DUBBING PROCESS DEMONSTRATES THE DIVERSE INTERPRETATIONS AND LANGUAGE ADAPTATIONS THAT CONTRIBUTE TO THE GLOBAL REACH AND ACCESSIBILITY OF FILMS, ALLOWING AUDIENCES AROUND THE WORLD TO ENGAGE WITH THE STORY AND CHARACTERS.

BERNARD HILL, KNOWN FOR HIS ROLE IN THE FILM, APPEARED IN THE TELEVISION SERIES FOX (1980), WHERE HE PORTRAYED THE SON OF PETER VAUGHAN'S CHARACTER. VAUGHAN, IN TURN, PLAYED DENETHOR IN THE BBC RADIO ADAPTATION OF THE LORD OF THE RINGS. THIS CONNECTION HIGHLIGHTS THE ACTORS' INVOLVEMENT IN DIFFERENT PROJECTS RELATED TO TOLKIEN'S WORK, FURTHER SHOWCASING THEIR VERSATILITY AND RANGE AS PERFORMERS.

-

FILMING THE ICONIC SCENE OF THE ROHIRRIM CHARGING THE PELENNOR REQUIRED A REMARKABLE FIFTY-TWO TAKES BEFORE THE CREW ACHIEVED THE DESIRED RESULT. THIS EXTENSIVE REPETITION DEMONSTRATES THE COMMITMENT AND DEDICATION OF THE FILMMAKERS TO CAPTURE THE INTENSITY AND GRANDEUR OF THE MOMENT, ENSURING THE HIGHEST QUALITY FOR THE FINAL PRODUCT.

-

THROUGHOUT THE FILMING PROCESS, APPROXIMATELY SIXTY OUT OF THE TOTAL TWO HUNDRED EIGHTY HORSES INVOLVED IN THE SCENE HAD TO BE REPLACED OR REMOVED DUE TO VARIOUS REASONS. THIS METICULOUS ATTENTION TO DETAIL HIGHLIGHTS THE PRIORITY PLACED ON ANIMAL WELFARE AND SAFETY DURING PRODUCTION, AS ANY CONCERNS OR ISSUES WERE PROMPTLY ADDRESSED TO ENSURE THE WELL-BEING OF THE ANIMALS.

-

LORD OF THE RINGS:

THE RETURN OF THE KING

ULTIMATE TRIVIA BOOK

TRIVIA, CURIOUS FACTS AND

BEHIND THE SCENES SECRETS

www.ingramcontent.com/pod-product-compliance
Lightning Source LLC
Chambersburg PA
CBHW071334140726
47996CB00005B/1966